Michelle Mayur (Australia), Compiling Author

Collaborators

Julie Ann (SINGAPORE)

Andrea Beadle (UNITED KINGDOM)

Raeline Brady (AUSTRALIA)

Rev. Lorraine Cohen (UNITED STATES)

Helaine Z. Harris (UNITED STATES)

Rev. Sage Taylor Kingsley-Goddard (UNITED STATES)

Christine Kloser (UNITED STATES)

Kerri Kannan (UNITED STATES)

Linda Murray (AUSTRALIA)

Joanne Newell (AUSTRALIA)

Jesse Ann Nichols George (UNITED STATES)

Janet Parsons (AUSTRALIA)

Brenda Pearce (CANADA)

Deb A. Scott (UNITED STATES)

Therese Skelly (UNITED STATES)

Rev. Edie Weinstein (UNITED STATES)

Praise for Embraced by the Divine

"If you're feeling alone, unloved or unsure, Embraced by the Divine will reach out and hug you, and let you know that you'll get through this. Be inspired by its stories of women just like you, who have overcome challenge or crisis by trusting in Spirit."

– FABIENNE FREDRICKSON, Founder of The Client Attraction Business School™ and Author of *Embrace Your Magnificence: Get out of your own way and live a fuller, richer, more abundant life*

"Embraced by the Divine is exactly how readers feel as they immerse themselves in these stories of faith, fortitude and freedom. Recognizing oneself in the story of another is the ultimate nod to the authenticity and heart the authors bring to these pages, and Michelle Mayur is to be commended for artfully gathering these incredible women who help us see ourselves more clearly through their words."

– SUE URDA, Co-Founder of Powerful You! Inc. www.powerfulyou.com

"An uplifting guide to finding hope, this is a beautiful book that I will return to again and again. I have found the stories resonant with light and love! An incredible gift to help those who are going through difficult times."

– JUDY O'BEIRN, Creator and Co-Author of Unwavering Strength, www.unwaveringstrength.com & www.hasmarkservices.com

"Loss of love. Loss of money. Loss of life. Loss of self. None of us are immune, but few have the courage to fearlessly embrace our cataclysms and dark storms like these authors have done. Each has, in her own way, gone into the abyss and come out the other side more whole and vitally alive than she ever could have imagined. Their stories seep straight down into those raw, cobwebby soul corners where we've always known that our greatness is born of the darkness."

– LISA MCCOURT, Bestselling Ghostwriter and Author of Hay House's *Juicy Joy – 7 Simple Steps to Your Glorious, Gutsy Self*

"Embraced by the Divine delivers on its promise. Reading the stories and guidance that these authentic, heart-centered, spiritually courageous women offer is a powerful path to healing and transformation."

– LORI LEYDEN, PhD, MBA, Trauma Healing Professional, Author, Speaker, Create Global Healing (CGH) and Project LIGHT: Rwanda. www.TappingSolutionFoundation.org

"I could not put this book down! I was immediately mesmerized by the brave, amazing women in Embraced by the Divine. Although from different continents, theirs is a story of commonality and community that we all share. They have courageously bared their hearts and souls to share their messages so that we may all grow from their experiences."

– SUZANNE DENK, Psy.D., Bestselling Author, *The Inner Circle Chronicles, 12 Intuitive Women Leaders of the New Economy, Transforming Lives and Businesses with Soul and Spirit*

"I found myself immediately drawn into and relating to so many of the author's stories – Yes, I've been there too – we all have! The authors are real, raw, and lay everything on the table. Through their triumphs we can find hope, inspiration and renewed sense of purpose."

— JEAN SLATTER, Author of *Hiring the Heavens*

"Juicy and often raw, these sisters are laying it all out to share their insights and experiences from deep within their hearts. Candid insights and sharing of life's challenges and lessons in a plethora of styles lead us to the silver lining meaning of it all. Well worth the read more than once!"

— AMBIKA DEVI, Creative Dreamer, Author of *Lilith*

"How beautiful to read and receive a collection of heart-focused women who by sharing their authentic, inspiring and at times painful stories can help us all heal and step into our own divine light. Loved it!"

— SHASTA TOWNSEND, Author of *Happy, Sexy, Shameless: What Your Mother Didn't Know About the Birds and the Bees*

"These are stories of 'normal' people who stepped up to their higher potential, moving forward even when it looked like they weren't going anywhere. This is a book of strength, faith, and responding to a higher call that I found deeply inspirational. A must read for anyone on the path of seeking and creating their best life."

— KAREN DRUCKER, Singer, Songwriter, Speaker, Author www.karendrucker.com

"Gaze into the heart of a woman and what you might find is joy, edged with pain, merged with love, intertwined with fear, with courage at the core. The women who share their stories in this empowering book, embody those qualities and more. As you read their words, you may find yourself nodding along, crying with them, applauding their fortitude and sharing the soul food from the plate that they offer to nourish your own hungry heart."

— GINI GENTRY, Bestselling Author *Dreaming Down Heaven*, a principle in Dreaming Heaven, Garden of the Goddess Retreat Center

"By lovingly sharing the insights and transformational tools they discovered through the process of facing their greatest challenges, the authors of Embraced by the Divine offer spiritual inspiration and practical guidance for any woman who is ready to fully embrace her highest potential in every aspect of her life."

— MALI APPLE AND JOE DUNN, Authors of *The Soulmate Experience: A Practical Guide to Creating Extraordinary Relationships* www.TheSoulmateExperience.com

EMBRACED BY THE DIVINE

THE EMERGING WOMAN'S GATEWAY TO POWER, PASSION AND PURPOSE

Michelle Mayur and friends

Foreword by Rev. Dr. Kimberly Marooney

www.EmbracedByTheDivine.com
michelle@embracedbythedivine.com

Cover image artwork Laurie Bain, Primal Painter, www.lightworkerenergyart.com
Cover design Charlotte Gelin Design and Photography, charlottegelin@yahoo.com.au

ISBN: 978-0-9941554-1-2

NOTE: Although there are contributing authors from four continents, for consistency the American Associated Press Stylebook grammar, spelling and punctuation are used throughout this book.

DISCLAIMER:

The views expressed by collaborators in reference to specific people in their chapter represent entirely their own individual opinions and are not in any way reflective of the views of Michelle Mayur, the compiling author. She assumes no responsibility for errors, omissions or contradictory interpretation of the subject matter herein. The compiling author does not warrant the performance, effectiveness, or applicability of any websites listed in or linked to this publication. The purchaser or reader of this publication assumes responsibility of the use of these materials and information. The compiling author shall in no event be held liable to any party for any direct, indirect, punitive, special, incidental, or any other consequential damages arising directly or indirectly from any use of this material. Techniques and processes given in this book are not to be used in place of medical advice.

Dedication

To Kalina and Michael, my two amazing children, who make me so proud to be their mother, inspiring me daily to help co-create a better world not only for them, but also for coming generations.

To women everywhere, who are no longer content to stand in the shadows, who are ready to reclaim their personal power and boldly step into and *own* their magnificence, turning their dreams into reality.

Table of Contents

Angel Blessing
Rev. Dr. Kimberly Marooney

Blessed one, we are here for you.

While your mind may question and doubt, we are here.

We are with you always, especially when you doubt.

Our presence is a blessing to you, just as your desire to connect with us is a blessing to all of creation.

We hold you in the heart of Divine Love.

We bathe you in comfort.

We drench you in peace.

We are here.

We stand behind you blessing you with protection and strength.

Can you feel our hands on your shoulders giving you comfort?

In our sacred embrace, it is safe to open your heart to love.

Love is the most precious gift we have to offer.

And yet, love is all there is.

You are composed of love.

The world around you is love.

It may not seem like that when you are feeling challenged and alone, but it is true.

The love of God – Divine Love – is all that truly matters.

Experiencing Divine Love is the greatest blessing one can receive.

Receive this blessing of love now.

In our embrace, open your heart to be filled by love.

Let this Divine Love satisfy your heart and soul.

Ask this Love to heal every wound.

Invite this outpouring of Divine Love to satisfy every desire.

Breathe into the expansion happening in your heart.

*Like a balloon getting bigger and bigger, let the Presence of
Love grow in your heart.*

*Let the love in your heart grow large enough to bless your family with
forgiveness, comfort, peace, joy, everything needed.*

*Let the love in your heart grow large enough to become a beacon of light for
your country and the Earth.*

How will you be a blessing to the people in your life?

All are connected through the heart, through love.

How can you shine?

Be the blessing that you are!

Gratitude
Michelle Mayur

My greatest thanks go to my parents, Miriam and Don Gilder, now guiding me from the other side. I offer heart-felt love and gratitude to my mother for introducing me to the beauty and healing power of Nature and for enriching my connection to Mother Earth. Thanks to my father for showing me by example that with passion and perseverance you can achieve your goals and live your dreams fully.

Special acknowledgment goes to my soul mate, Dr. Rashmi Mayur. Our time together was brief before his untimely passing, but our life together was rich with spiritual adventures and love. He taught me by example, through his work at the United Nations, that no matter what your circumstances or challenges, you always have the potential to act both locally and globally to positively impact the lives of others and to care for Mother Earth.

Naturally, without the transformational contributions to this book of my wonderful collaborator Soul Sisters – some of the most inspirational women on the planet today – this book would not have been possible. I feel so honored and blessed to have been chosen by the higher realms to bring this book forth into physical form. Some of these collaborators, such as Christine Kloser and Raeline Brady, have been both mentors and friends to me. Other gifted souls, such as Janet Parsons and Linda Murray, I have had the privilege of working with to bring their gifts out into the world.

Special mention must go to my dear friend Rev. Lorraine Cohen. Despite being on opposite sides of the world, the bond between us has continued to grow stronger and stronger as we share, support and nurture each other in that ongoing journey to self-mastery.

I honor and bless all those people who have inspired me to think outside the box, who have believed in me (sometimes more than I have believed in myself), who have helped me to find the strength within to follow my dreams and who have been there for me to help me pick myself up and dust myself off when things haven't gone according to my plan. Thank you to everyone who has believed in me and in the vision for this book.

Special Gratitude to Our Sponsors

I feel honored to have BEST PRACTICE BUSINESS SCHOOL www.bestpracticebusinesscoaching.com.au as the book's MAJOR SPONSOR.

You can read more about their training programs
at the end of this book.

Thank you to everyone who has contributed financially at the Bronze, Silver and Gold levels to making this book possible and for helping to spread its messages of love, courage and hope to women around the world.

Deep Gratitude goes to our Platinum Sponsor Anita B. from Singapore and to our Diamond Sponsor Rose Hoyt from Australia.

Foreword
– Rev. Dr. Kimberly Marooney

Trust. Trust. Trust.

That is what I hear my heart saying when I don't know what to do. Trust. I hear that little voice in my heart telling me to trust as I write to you. Trust that the words I am writing are the ones your heart and soul need to hear at this moment.

This book is in your hands because your soul guided you to it. Each woman who contributed found a way to trust that the story she had to tell, the wisdom gained through experience, and the tools or remedies that worked for her will serve you, too. Each contributor found a place of trust within herself that lifted her up to a higher consciousness of love, power, passion and transformation that allowed miracles to happen.

So trust. Trust that you are being guided this very moment by your soul, angels, the Divine, Holy Spirit, God. You are not alone. You are never alone. Your team of spiritual beings is with you always providing the love, support, comfort, guidance and resources you need each moment of life. Trust that is so.

If you close your eyes, put a hand on your heart, take a breath and drop inside yourself, can you feel the love surrounding you and filling your heart? It is real. The love is present, whether you notice it or not. The love is there no matter what your situation.

Sometimes we think we imagined an experience of connection like a tender caress by a breeze on your cheek, goose bumps rippling through your body as a "knowing" pops into your awareness, or an empowering surge of energy. In the moment, we know it is real and true. A moment later, our minds judge and tell us that we made it up. We imagined it. We are not worthy of direct contact with the Divine. THAT is the imagined story.

We are worthy of true Love. We are worthy of direct communion with God, angels and spiritual beings. We don't need to earn or deserve that connection. It is present ALWAYS.

Our job is to trust – to lean into Spirit, both in moments of need and moments of joy. To find that small, inner voice that speaks truth and conveys knowing. To trust.

Thank God that Michelle Mayur trusted the request she received to co-create *Embraced by the Divine*. The angels called her and she said, "Yes!" It has taken tremendous trust, courage, fortitude, and determination for Michelle to create this gift of love now in your hands. She has benefited beyond measure from the experience. I have watched her blossom into so much more of who she truly is with each step of this creation.

Michelle called me, and each of the women who contributed powerful chapters, to tell our stories of heartache, pain, and hope as we faced extraordinary challenges. We trusted the call and said, "Yes." We harvested the wisdom of our personal transformation to stand courageously in the light of love as beacons for you to follow.

How are you being challenged by life?

How is Spirit calling you to trust?

What are you deeply passionate about?

We pray that the stories in this book provide what you need each moment of your journey into trust and transformation as your strengths and abilities are forged in the fire of life.

You are an extraordinary person. You are a Child of Light. You are loved, and you are loving. You possess divine soul qualities, special abilities, and unique wisdom. You are treasured and loved. Your team of angels and spiritual beings are holding you in that love this very moment. Can you feel it? Trust. This love is real and present.

Trust.

You need not try to make anything happen right now. Spirit is here, holding you in love. Receive the gifts of healing and comfort offered.

God wants you to be everything you were intended to be. A brilliant, beautiful being, radiating love. Situated in truth. Emanating grace. Steeped in eternal peace. Ready, willing, and able to serve. A vibrant, joyful powerful woman [man] in the world. A tender, sensual, and compassionate lover. A devoted, humble, and sincere companion. God wants you to unite with other souls to revel in the miracles and magnificence of union. Giving, trusting, and thriving.

Each story you read is an open invitation. Read the story as if it was written personally for you. It was! Feel your friendship, your connection with the writer grow as you read. Unite with her. Experience her insight, courage, and strength flow into you. Read her bio. Visit her website. Receive the gifts of grace, wisdom, love and healing she is offering.

Reach out! Actually connect! Send an email of gratitude telling her how you benefited from her story. We want to hear from you! Michelle and I want to hear from you, too.

In this way, you go beyond the mind to be "Embraced by the Divine." You are taking to heart the energy of love. You are taking action to change, to move, to transform. You are raising your vibration to a higher frequency with these actions.

In this higher frequency, you will discover your own wisdom, love and resources. This is where miracles happen as you are personally embraced by the Divine. We pray that you, in turn, share the love and miracles you receive.

You are just as extraordinary. You are the treasure. Say, "Yes" to the calling of your soul and shine brightly. Trust.

With much love,
Kimberly

REV. DR. KIMBERLY MAROONEY is the beloved author of *Angel Blessings Cards*. She is a beautiful spirit who lifts up the souls who come to her, deepening their hearts to know the Divine Creator within. Blessed with the ability to experience direct, personal union with God, angels and Spiritual Beings, Kimberly has authored a dozen bestselling books, founded the Angel Ministry, and hosted the Archangel Activations. Visit KIMBERLYMAROONEY.COM

Introduction
– Michelle Mayur

I well remember the first time I met the Deputy Prime Minister of Australia at a function. He came up smiling and bent his tall frame down to say hello to my little daughter. In my nervousness, I blurted out something completely incomprehensible, not only to him, but also to me!

It was back in the days when I still placed successful people up on a pedestal and myself much lower down the scale – a relative nobody. It felt to me like some were born to reach great heights, while others were pre-destined to remain in mediocrity, or even worse. Call it a belief in Fate, if you will.

Although passionate about self-help and my spiritual path for many years, I still believed that I could only aspire to reach my smaller dreams, constrained by my position in life. After all, what hope did a divorced 40-something, financially challenged mother of two have to make a big difference in the world? Of course, being a great mother and raising two healthy, well-adjusted children is a pretty full-on job, so any other dreams of mine just went onto the backburner. I was totally out of my power, neglecting myself and always putting others first. As a woman, I know I was not unique in these feelings.

However, something burned deep inside. My narrow comfort zone was getting increasingly uncomfortable. I felt like a prisoner. Was it really conceivable that I could aspire to greater heights? My soul was calling me and was not about to rest. The excuses I had been using to stay stuck in limiting beliefs were starting to sound hollow. You know, the divorced mother thing, being too old, not enough money, not feeling good enough and so on and so forth. The list of excuses to continue playing small had seemed endless…

I immersed myself in books and in intellectualizing deeper spiritual truths such as we are all connected as one energetically. Full of admiration for these inspirational authors, bit by bit I began to realize that so many leaders in the fields of human potential, self-help and spirituality had first had to overcome many major hurdles and challenges to get to the successful place they now enjoyed. Bankruptcy, losing their house, divorce, death of a child, being scorned and misunderstood, facing cancer and so on seemed to be occurring in this select group far more frequently than in the general population. It began to dawn on me that many of the people I admired most, and who now seemed to have it all, had actually had a really tough journey to get there, but had never given up, despite all the challenges thrown in their way. My own excuses for playing small now looked pretty weak.

Fast-forward a few years to a major energetic shift for me in Egypt, which you can read about later on in the book, and I committed to playing a much bigger game. Luckily, you don't have to go all the way to Egypt to step into your power and make a bigger difference in the world, or even just in your local community. The possibilities are endless.

Written by Light-filled, inspirational women across four continents, the juicy chapters in this book are all deliberately raw, vulnerable and authentic. No pretense or false personas here. Many of these high-vibration Soul Sisters are already big names on the world stage and the other collaborators are close behind, so it is an honor and a blessing to have been able to bring them together so easily.

I shouldn't really be surprised, though, because the angels guided me to write this book. One sunny summer morning as I was peacefully watering my garden, they told me clearly that I should write a compilation book, calling it *Embraced by the Divine*. They also told me this book should inspire women to reclaim their personal power, own their talents and gifts and be part of the new wave of women bringing in the empowered feminine energies of Love and Compassion.

These true stories of hope, courage and transformation cover a broad spectrum of challenges and obstacles that our contributors have personally overcome, including: bankruptcy, messy divorce, death of a child, fearing "not being good enough," chronic anxiety, drugs, death of a special pet, and surviving breast cancer and other severe health challenges. The one common thread is that these apparently negative life experiences have contained within them a gift that has made all these women stronger and more passionate about helping and inspiring others.

You are likely to both laugh and cry as you engage in the powerful true stories of these Light-filled women. Many times, you will find the collaborator has already been where you are at now, whether it is financial difficulties, tortured relationships, severe health challenges, grief or just plain feeling stuck. Even when it seemed like there was no way out, these amazing women found the unexpected blessing in the ordeal.

Each collaborator also shares some of the rich tapestry of tools and processes that helped her not only to overcome her major challenges, but to go on to realize her dreams, often in far bigger ways than she had ever imagined!

Definition of Divine

The word *Divine* has been used throughout this book in a broad spiritual sense and not as part of any religious dogma. You are free to insert whatever term you resonate with, such as Source, God, Angels, The One, Creator, Buddha, Spirit, Jesus, Divine Mother and so on.

How to Use This Book

THIS BOOK IS A TRANSFORMATIONAL EXPERIENCE. Trust that it is no coincidence you have been drawn to it. Your time for change is now, right down to the level of your DNA. There are many messages contained within the pages of this book that have the potential to transform your life into greater happiness and joy and into doing the work you love.

You may like to just read this book from cover to cover and enjoy a really juicy, inspirational read. You can also pick the chapters that you are most drawn to from the Table of Contents page. You may even like to simply let the book fall open at a particular page, trusting that this will be part of the chapter you need to read at the time, probably because there are words and messages that will act as triggers for your own healing and inspiration.

This book has truly been a labor of love. Each time you read it you will find even deeper levels of meaning and wisdom contained within the pages. It is a tool to help you to grow into all that you can be.

All the collaborators and I invite you to also connect with us via our websites and social media. We welcome the opportunity to be of service and support in your personal journey.

With love,

Michelle

Who Am I to Shine?

– Michelle Mayur

"God doesn't call the qualified, he qualifies the called."
~ Rev. Michael Beckwith

Recalibration in Egypt

The second of December 2007, a very special day in history, well at least in my own personal history. That day my world changed forever as I was reborn into a higher-vibration version of myself.

It all seems so surreal now looking back to that day in the King's Chamber of the Great Pyramid on the Giza Plateau in Egypt. I was facilitating one of my Spiritual Egypt Tours with an exceptional group of healers. Each of us had a deep inner knowing that we had been drawn to Egypt for far greater reasons than mere happy snaps in front of the pyramids. We were there as Lightworkers healing the planet, even if consciously we didn't know quite how we were to do it.

We had already each had profound mystical experiences as we journeyed along the Nile from south to north, visiting all the major temples and having private time in many of them. The energies in these ancient temples are so intense they are indescribable, forcing you to confront and release that which no longer serves you.

In all honesty, after nearly three weeks of travel in Egypt, by the time we reached the Sphinx and the pyramids on the Giza Plateau we were all feeling a little jaded and our resistance to holding onto the outmoded old was low. It had been one spiritual adventure after another, with many Divine Synchronicities as well as a touch of Divine Magic.

We soon found out that when you are called to do work to benefit (wo)mankind in alignment with your Divine Mission, the higher realms step in and lend a helping hand.

Anyone who has ever visited the Giza Plateau in Egypt will know that it is usually crawling with thousands of tourists from sunrise to sunset, all jostling for that perfect photo opportunity.

It still leaves me in absolute awe when I remember our private group having the ENTIRE Giza Plateau to ourselves for two whole hours! We had free access to the Great Pyramid and the Sphinx for as long as we wanted, allowing us to receive any initiations we were ready for and doing our planetary healing work as intuited.

Well you may ask how we managed to manifest this. Seems our tour guide's brother was the Chief Inspector of the Giza Plateau, so with a bit of negotiation between the two brothers we had free reign of the whole plateau. Talk about Divine Synchronicity! The guards on camelback surrounding the perimeter were all a-buzz trying to figure out who we were, since such luxuries were something usually reserved only for royalty and presidents!

It was important to the higher realms that we did our planetary healing work undisturbed by the clamor of tourists. The immensely powerful toning of Siriun Light Language from a diminutive lady in our group reverberated throughout the King's Chamber all the way back down to the entrance of the Great Pyramid. Another lady did advanced crystal grid work. Many of us channeled energy and sat in prayer and meditation. Some brave souls, myself included, received an initiation lying in the empty stone sarcophagus in the King's Chamber.

Spiraling higher and higher, the combined energies rose to a crescendo, to an intensity that felt as if our whole neural circuitry had been blown apart. We were being recalibrated from the ground up. Nothing would ever be the same again … and it hasn't been!

The Holy 2 x 4

It took several weeks after returning to my home in Melbourne before I felt able to function properly and was firmly back on planet Earth again. Everything had changed and I knew my healing work was to undergo a radical shift. No more suburban healing practitioner. Intuitively I knew the Divine had much higher plans for me. Pity though, that I didn't have any clue what form this new work would take.

Knowing what I know now, I could have saved myself a whole lot of struggle, uncertainty, frustration and money in searching for that elusive something if I had only stopped the busy-ness and spent more time in prayer and meditation, asking the *Divine* to guide me step-by-step in what I was to do next. Instead, over the next two years I dabbled in this, I did a little bit of that, got further qualifications, got exhausted and burnt out. Still I felt no closer to finding that elusive work that I was to be doing. "Why wasn't I getting any help or guidance?" I lamented.

All I knew was that I was miserable, doing much unfulfilling work. I desperately wanted to retreat from the whole world – family and friends included – for at least six months, just to regain my energy. Seemed I just needed a break. (Careful what you wish for!)

In my busy-ness and struggle to figure things out with my ego mind I was actually standing in my own way. Seems the higher realms had been progressively giving me a number of gentle nudges that I had been too busy to notice, trying to bring me into alignment with my Divine Mission. Eventually nothing less than the *Holy 2x4* was needed to gain my attention!

Driving back along the freeway from a friend's place in late 2009, I noticed the car number-plate in front of me was *WAK*. Ooh, that got my attention. (Messages on car number-plates are one of the common ways angels communicate with me, weird as that may sound.) Perhaps it was a warning of an impending crash, so I slowed right down and was extra careful. Nothing. Arriving home safely, I pondered the significance of seeing *WAK*.

It didn't take me too long to find out! Within an hour of arriving home, I suddenly slipped on the kitchen floor and fell *WACK* onto my right shoulder, breaking it badly. Well, that was going to put me out of action for a while. Being self-employed and a single parent, that was a scary thought as financially we lived pretty much from week to week. Seems I really got that "break" I so desperately wanted! Could I go back and rephrase that please?

In a cubicle by myself in the emergency department of the local hospital, I was waiting for the results of the X-rays, pretty much a foregone conclusion. Suddenly the whole cubicle lit up in intense violet Light and I knew the angels were with me. Of course, I knew my "accident" had nothing to do with bad luck and that everything was being divinely orchestrated from above. "Angels," I said, "I don't know why breaking my shoulder was necessary, but please support me through this financially."

My prayers were answered. Although unable to work properly for the next three months, I received two sizeable and unexpected checks, one for a tax refund I wasn't expecting and another for underpaid Family Allowance from the Government. Together they covered roughly what I would have made seeing clients for that period!

Now I'll let you in on a little secret. As a professional energy healer for roughly 14 years then, my ego mind was telling me I should be able to do a few energy treatments on my shoulder, work through any related emotional issues or past life issues and be up and running in no time. However the higher realms wanted to ensure I wasn't tempted to revert back to the old things I had been doing that had burnt me out, so I was forced to eat some humble pie and resign myself to the healing being much slower than I would have liked it to be.

The Seed of Heal the Healer Is Planted

So here I was, several doors now firmly shut behind me, waiting for that elusive new door that I hoped was just about to open. Because my shoulder was taking so long to heal, I jokingly kept saying to my friends, "It's a case of Healer Heal Thyself!" Maybe that too was an angel message?

I'd always naturally attracted a high number of healers as private clients. What if I could reach many, many more healers around the world and make a bigger impact? In fact, what if I could use my 14 years' experience as a healing professional to help other healers fast track their healing practices to success? Certainly I had a wealth of experience in what NOT to do in terms of marketing, as well as having much practical experience in doing the all-important Inner Work and in building a tribe of satisfied clients. The seed of Heal the Healer germinated and the door opened a crack.

Little did I realize at the time all the fears and challenges I would face in getting Heal the Healer up and running into a successful online community and business. Little could I imagine about the layers and layers of frightened Inner Child parts that would arise for healing, the expensive technological challenges and the multiple steep learning curves. Still that little voice inside me – my connection to the Divine – kept encouraging me to continue, despite all the setbacks and obstacles in my path. It would have been so easy to quit, throw in the towel and go back to just being a suburban healing practitioner. However, if I gave in to those feelings of frustration and fear and just quit, I know a part of my soul would have died too, along with my dream of helping healers around the world to excel.

Let's face it, I knew absolutely *nothing* about running an online business. Sure I had a website, but I really didn't have a clue about selling things online. In fact, I really couldn't abide those super-long sales pages filled with false promises and marketing hype. After all, I was a Healer, not a Marketer. How on earth was I going to create a global business online? It all seemed so overwhelming. Was I really crazy for dreaming so big?

I needed help! My skillset was hopelessly inadequate for the task at hand. I decided to learn as much as I could about marketing (yuck!), employ the services of a highly recommended marketer – co-incidentally also one of my Reiki students many years before – and get someone to help me construct a membership website with all the bells and whistles for Heal the Healer. I was just going to plunge in headfirst. Well perhaps it was actually more like teeter precariously on the edge before eventually falling in and having to sink or swim.

Six months into Heal the Healer and the website designer was finding the task of building a membership website well beyond the capacity of the platform he had chosen. It just wasn't going to work, despite all the money I had already put into it. The credit card was already taking a severe battering, but I viewed it as an investment that would *eventually* pay huge returns.

Learning to Surrender to the Divine

I was referred to someone else to help me get the membership website up and running, but she came back with a quote for $8,000! It was at that point I just broke down sobbing on my knees, "God, I thought you wanted me to do this. I thought you wanted me to help other healers take their work to new heights. If you really want me to do this, PLEASE HELP! Show me the way. I can't do this alone." It was at that point that I SURRENDERED completely to the Divine and stopped trying to struggle and figure things out by myself. This was probably the single most powerful thing I could have done. (These days I surrender to the Divine and ask for help and guidance in my daily meditations, without ever needing to reach that desperation point.)

Fifteen minutes later, I was guided to Google something and the name of a web programmer "jumped out" at me. He specialized in creating exactly the kind of membership website I was after. Fifteen minutes after that we were having a conversation. Not only did he finish up literally being a Godsend for me in creating the website, but he was also a fabulous mentor on all the technical stuff I needed to master.

Self-Doubt and Layers of Fear

Now for the next major challenge: ME! Since childhood I had been painfully shy and usually hid in the background. I was still carrying the trauma from Year 8 at school when I had to give a five-minute impromptu presentation about teachers in front of my English class. I vividly remember standing on the dais too petrified to even speak a word for the *entire* five minutes, which incidentally felt like a lifetime. Now I needed to start speaking live to large groups of people online. Are you kidding me?

My marketing man had come up with a brilliant plan to launch the Heal the Healer community: a telesummit called Breakthrough to Abundance for Healers. Talk about falling in the deep end! Not only was I unknown to the big-name speakers I wanted to attract, but I'd never even interviewed anyone before, let alone in front of possibly thousands of people! Serious self-doubt was kicking in. Make that absolute terror. I definitely felt I'd bitten off WAY more than I could chew.

That overwhelming fear showed up as procrastination. To invite the big-name speakers to speak at my launch event, my marketing man wanted me to make individual, customized video invitations so they could actually see me and not just receive a written email.

It amazes me now that I ever completed those customized videos. Four months in and I was still making every excuse under the sun and finding other things to distract myself with in order not to face my fear of making these darned videos. The lighting wasn't right, the background was too busy, I needed to lose some kilos first, my script wasn't good enough, I needed a better video camera, blah, blah, blah.

It came as a total surprise when I actually got more speakers than I needed saying "Yes."

Who was I to position myself as an expert? That fear of not being good enough reared its ugly head again, something that was going to happen multiple times as I continued to shift vibrationally and take my work to higher levels. To me, it didn't seem important enough that I had immersed myself in listening to as many relevant teleseminars as possible, had researched and read salient articles and had done lots of my own inner work so I could really claim the title of being an expert for healers. Seemed my fear-based perfectionist tendencies still needed a lot more work.

As I was such a newbie to online marketing, creating teleseminars, shopping carts, autoresponders, social media, etc., etc., I put my full faith and trust in other more experienced people to guide me. I realize now that my faith and trust would have been better directed towards the Divine and in trusting the loving guidance of the higher realms. In retrospect, it would have saved me a whole lot of heartache. My marketing guy had a particular vision for Heal the Healer, based primarily on teaching healers how to build a lucrative healing business. However something felt misaligned. Was it my gut instinct or was that just my own fear holding me back? I couldn't tell. That would have been a really good time to have spent more time in prayer and meditation so I could have received the Divine Guidance that the concept was indeed a vibrational mismatch for me and that my gut feeling was right.

I did my vision board for success, wrote my desire statement in detail and said affirmations. It was all stuff to appease the conscious mind and did little if anything to address limiting beliefs locked securely into the subconscious, the 90 percent of the mind that runs our patterns and habits. The desired result of the telesummit launch event I envisaged was hundreds of people signing up as paying members of Heal the Healer. After all, I'd done everything right – or so I thought – so why shouldn't I enjoy enormous success?

The telesummit was a huge success and I got rave reviews about it. Even the speakers commented on how professional I was as a host. (What is that about "fake it till you make it?") Of course, there were still some technical glitches, like the phone line dropping out while one speaker was leading a beautiful guided meditation. Neither she nor I knew anything had happened at first, so there she was continuing her meditation in cyberspace while I had to clumsily improvise and fill in until such time as she realized and got back on the phone line!

But I Wanted It in the Big Square Box with the Red Ribbon...

After the event I waited for the membership signups, expecting them to roll in. Instead, I got just a handful. I had been so attached to a particular outcome coming in a particular package and this definitely wasn't it. Why not? I had done everything by the book. What had I done wrong? It seemed like the worst personal failure I could have imagined at the time. I had been counting on an influx of recurring membership fees to start to bring down that $20,000 plus credit card debt that had accrued from birthing Heal the Healer.

Actually, it was a divine blessing in disguise, although it definitely didn't feel like it at the time. All my hopes and dreams shattered, then followed closely by my Dark Night of the Soul. It was just before Christmas and I vividly remember the numbness and total disconnection I felt from everyone and everything. Bouts of gut-wrenching sobbing were the only things that broke my numbness. Why had God and the angels failed me? Didn't they want me to succeed? I withdrew deeper and deeper inwards. The feelings of utter failure and devastation were just too much to bear. Why had I even bothered trying to create Heal the Healer? Who was I to shine and realize my dream of helping healers around the world? Had the whole idea just been a delusion of my ego?

Learning to be Held in the Embrace of the Divine

Sometimes we need to go right down into the pit of despair in order to surrender our need to control and try to "fix" things or work things out. We just need to let God and let go. I had no fight or resistance to "letting go" left in me. I surrendered to the Divine. All I wanted to do was to be held safe, supported and nurtured in the arms of the Divine Mother. I found myself imagining being held in her arms like a young child with my head on her warm nurturing breast, feeling safe and loved. Angels were all around us, beaming unconditional love to me. I felt myself releasing all the tension in my muscles, nerves, bones and blood vessels, being *embraced by the Divine* and surrendering to Divine Love.

For several weeks or more, I continued to ask to be held in the arms of the Divine Mother multiple times each day, especially when I went to bed at night. That was when the shift started up from the bottom of the Dark Night of the Soul. Slow at first, but then I was in a space to ask, "What next? What is it that I am really supposed to be doing now?"

Learning to Step Out of My Own Way

You know when you are tapped in to Divine Guidance. It is gentle, comforting and never harsh. Often you receive the answer before you even finish asking the question. The answers now started to come easily, as I was open and receptive from having spent so much time alone in stillness and in nature. Yes, I had been right all along and should have trusted my gut instinct. Heal the Healer had not been the right fit and the Divine had blocked me from wasting any more time pursuing something that was misaligned. If I had had lots of paid membership signups as a result of the launch event, I would have kept going down that track and would not have been open to being re-directed onto the right path for me.

There was still that ego part of me that baulked at the idea of changing everything in Heal the Healer around to free membership and to focusing on helping healers win their Inner Game, rather than just doing the "building your healing business" side. The shift was definitely in the spiritual direction, moving from the by-line of "Health, Wealth and Happiness" to "Reclaiming Your Divine Light." Phew, finally that was authentically me and it fitted like a glove.

Since then Heal the Healer has continued to go from strength to strength. It only took roughly a year to have members from more than 100 countries. That still blows me away. I have been able to build a network of friends and colleagues around the world, all fulfilling our dream of helping raise the consciousness of humanity. No longer do I fear public speaking as I've spoken on and hosted so many teleseminars that it has become second nature. No longer do I procrastinate for days about sending out a newsletter or email broadcast. I don't worry anymore about how others will judge me, as everyone sees things through their own respective filters. There is no need to try to emulate someone else. People are drawn to me because of my authenticity. Not everyone likes me or gets where I am coming from and now I am comfortable with that.

Heal the Healer will continue to evolve as I do. At least now I have learned to trust the guidance of the Divine in every decision I make. No longer do I value the advice of "expert" people with their hidden agendas, subconscious or otherwise, above the guidance of the Divine, which always comes from a place of Love.

There is nothing we could ever have said or done that will change God's Love for us. Even if you fall down while pursuing your dreams, remember you can always call on the Divine to pick you up, dust you off and set you on the right track!

Fun Things to Play With to Deepen Your Connection to Divine Guidance

DAILY PRAYER SUGGESTION

"God, how best may I serve and be abundantly paid for doing so? Please show me a divinely aligned action step to take today. Please make it very clear." *(The time, energy and money I could have saved if I had started using this prayer much sooner!)*

SPEND MORE TIME IN PRAYER AND MEDITATION

Especially in beautiful places in nature, you are naturally closer to the Divine. The voice of the Divine is much easier to hear in the stillness. One hour spent in BE-ING is ultimately often far more valuable and productive than several hours spent in ego-mind DO-ING.

RECLAIM YOUR POWER

Say these words out loud, really feeling into them as you say them:

"I AM the Power and Presence of God.

I AM Divine Love.

I choose to reclaim my power now

From everyone and everything I have ever given it away to,

In this lifetime or any other

Through every level and dimension of my being.

I choose to reclaim my power now.

I feel my power flowing back to me.

I feel my power SURGING back to me.

(Pause and really feel your power coming back into your core column of Light, just in front of your spine. You may also notice your energy field expanding.)

I AM Divine Love.

I feel Divine Love flowing in, through and as me.

And so be it and it is done!

DIVINE MOTHER MEDITATION

Imagine yourself like a small child lying in the arms of the Divine Mother with your head resting on her nurturing breast, safe and warm. You may also see or sense the presence of angels surrounding you, all beaming unconditional love to you. Feel yourself relaxing more and more as you easily surrender your stresses, fears and worries to the Divine Mother. Feel yourself embraced by the Divine. Enjoy often, especially when you go to bed at night. Perfect for when you need to feel safe and comforted.

PRACTICE CONNECTING TO THE ANGELS BY ASKING THEM QUESTIONS

The voice of the angels is always gentle, reassuring and filled with loving guidance. In a quiet place, ask the angels a question. If the answer comes back even before you have finished asking the question, then it is higher truth. If however there is a gap of a couple of seconds before you receive the answer, know that your ego mind has substituted something so you don't look silly!

MICHELLE MAYUR (AUSTRALIA), in partnership with the Divine, co-creates transformational energetic shifts in women who are ready to make a bigger difference in the world. Through both her writing and her healing work, she assists women to dissolve limiting beliefs and energetic blockages so they can step fully into their Power, Passion and Purpose. She is the founder of the Heal the Healer community, WWW.HEAL-THE-HEALER.COM. Since 1995, Michelle has been running her successful healing practice, Angel Wings Healing, WWW.ANGELWINGS-HEALING.COM, seeing clients around the world,

Getting Raw –
Bungee Jumping into the Abyss
– Rev. Lorraine Cohen

"Enlightenment is a destructive process. It has nothing to do with becoming better or being happier. Enlightenment is the crumbling away of untruth. It's seeing through the facade of pretense. It's the complete eradication of everything we imagined to be true."
~ Adyashanti

I'm often asked how I began my spiritual journey. My answer always is … my mother died. I've been intuitive, psychic and somewhat aware for most of my life and my mother's death in 1981 was a catalyst for me to begin a deeper conscious awakening. Saying goodbye to her at a young age of 66 to leukemia and other complications broke my heart.

It's not unusual for a traumatic or dramatic event to lead you to question, "Why am I here? What is my purpose? What is life all about?"

At that time, I was living in New York City as an account executive for a well-known accessories company on Fifth Avenue and after her death my life began to fall apart.

One night I experienced a spiritual earthquake. I had a vision of myself standing in rubble. All the walls that had protected me from knowing myself had crumbled, at least the ones I was ready to see. I remember thinking how full of crap I was. I was a stranger to myself, hiding behind so many masks, lies, anger, and shame.

Help! I've fallen and I can't get up.

I felt raw, alone, and scared…"Who am I?"

I fell to my knees and for the first time I prayed to God for help and committed to walk in the Light, no matter what. It was time to find ME with the Grace of God to guide me.

I had no idea what the answer to my prayer would be.

My journey of courage, faith, and trust was beginning. My life would never be the same…

Pay Attention to What You Ask For

I began to read as many books and teachings on spirituality that I could find and a new world broke open for me. One book was Shirley MacLaine's, *Out on a Limb*. As I read, I felt my heart tremble with excitement and I sobbed as some of my questions were answered. I began meeting others on a spiritual path. New friends, mentors and teachers helped me to see myself and my life through fresh eyes.

My time in New York had come to an end and in 1986 I took a leap of faith and moved to Pennsylvania to begin the next chapter of my life. It was totally unknown. I became a hypnotherapist, an addictions counselor, psychotherapist and energy healer. Following this path also led me to become a Rev. Dr. interfaith minister. My life was exploding with possibilities!

I began working in a recovery center as a therapist with some of the most courageous people I have ever known. They taught me about the capacity of the human heart and spirit to cope with and survive life's most painful experiences. Their courage to face their deepest wounds gave me the strength and courage to face many of mine.

My therapy practice was booming. People were on a waiting list to work with me. My expertise was focused on inner child healing, releasing emotional pain, and helping people connect more deeply with their spirit.

Each week I counseled and led therapy sessions with more than 100 people and while their breakthroughs and growth were a privilege to facilitate and witness, I was feeling burned out from the intense pain and the horrific stories people shared. The thought of doing this deeply painful work for the next five, 10, or 20 years was daunting.

If I stopped doing therapy work, what would I do?

I realized that I had been coaching people in counseling sessions and decided making this shift was a natural choice. So I said yes and began taking steps to segue my business.

When One Door Closes…

Within months my practice began shrinking for no apparent reason. I had just bought a new house, new car, remodeled the basement for client sessions, and my income began a steady decline. My life was falling apart again.

This was one of the darkest times of my life. I felt a duality within myself, experiencing my human feelings of terror, worry, and pain and the peace and calm from my soul saying, *"All is well."* I was on an emotional rollercoaster that was dismantling many of my defenses and bringing me to my knees. I was fighting to hold on and learning how to surrender at the same time.

Intuitively, I knew I was being taught how to transform fear into courage, faith and power and to deepen my connection with God. I also knew that I was being trained to teach and guide others how to do the same; to walk through the darkness into Light with passion, purpose, and POWER.

I prayed for help. "Dear God. Help me stay strong and walk through this with me."

"Stop fighting child. Let go and let me carry you."

"I don't know how."

"I will teach you."

I knew I had created this life-changing experience for my own healing, growth and spiritual evolution and I felt grateful for the gift. When the darkness lifted, I felt stronger and more connected to Source than ever. I had learned critical keys to strengthen my inner foundation of faith and trust with God, to turn insecurity to confidence, and doubt/fear to courage.

Life is a journey of courage full of bumps, twists and turns, and ups and downs that repeatedly stretch you out of your comfort zone. If everything stayed the same day in and day out, imagine where the world would be today.

When you make a prayer the Universe listens and instantly responds. Often the form that response takes is very different from what you expect and want. Loving assistance always brings the experience that serves your best and highest good.

Your life can change in an instant! I've had periods that seemed magical with ease, grace, and abundant flow. I've had times of deep pain and suffering, scarcity, and lack that made my life feel hard and hopeless. And I have felt alone, lost, and disconnected from God.

So, at the end of 2010 I made a powerful prayer: to be taught how to stand in unshakeable faith, and trust and to know and feel God's love.

YIKES!!!

I didn't realize the magnitude of that request and the events that would follow to fulfill my wish.

For years I had heard and taught that God is the Source of all our good and that we need to lean on this Presence to take care of our wants and needs. I've had tons of evidence of divine intervention and yet the fear and distrust was still alive in me.

What I came to understand is the vital importance of having a strong bond with whoever you call God.

I wanted to know and feel God's love. I needed to know that I could trust God to take care of me no matter what.

The answers began to come…

Debts mounted, my business was not doing well and I felt myself and my life slowly unraveling again. I fell to my knees as my heart broke open and I sank into fear, doubt and feelings of unworthiness and helplessness with the weight of emotional burdens I had been carrying for years.

What would happen next?

What Doesn't Kill You Makes You Stronger

"Lorraine, you have breast cancer."

Huh? Seriously?

I felt no fear or worry. I was calm even though I was in-between health insurance.

I knew there was an emotional connection to my creating cancer. The message my heart had been trying to communicate revealed repressed feelings of unforgiveness, anger, guilt, helplessness towards myself, my mother, God and others…

Before I even asked God for help, the miracles began to happen. All of my medical bills were completely paid for, I had the best doctors at one of the most prestigious hospitals in the region, friends offered healing sessions and help for anything I needed, I received a grant for $2,000 worth of alternative therapies including yoga, massage, and acupuncture. And the gifts and blessings kept coming.

I felt wrapped in love.

I chose to only have a lumpectomy and follow my guidance to decline chemo, radiation, and Tamoxifen. I walked through the experience with courage, faith and trust into health, with the Universe supporting me.

Breathe … surrender…

Breathe some more … slowly … and deeply…

Sometimes you must have a break-down before you have a break-through…

2012 was a momentous year in ushering in a New Age. Having upheavals in your life that lift you to new heights of consciousness or bring you to your knees is part of the process that opens doors to new possibilities.

Before the year ended, my sweet 14-year old cat Wesley made transition on 11:11 at 11:30 am. I cried every day for that month as he slowly slipped away and my heart broke open again.

Throughout 2012 I noticed a significant shift happening within me. I felt a stronger connection with my soul and the Divine. I felt more inner peace and happiness for no reason. Fear had dramatically loosened its grip on my heart and mind when I was connected to my center and taking good care of myself – body, mind, and spirit.

There were times I felt myself watching what was happening in my life as an observer and witness, which was fascinating.

As I was becoming more present in my body and the NOW it was eye-opening to see how often I felt I was surrendering – letting God and letting go when I was really in resistance. I could feel the stress in my neck and shoulders, the desire to eat something, or the anger that erupted when I resisted what is.

Letting Go

"Surrender doesn't mean giving up. It means knowing when you have done enough and it's time to let God and let go"
~ Lorraine Cohen

I had a light-bulb moment. I don't know how to surrender and turn it over. How can I stand in unshakeable courage, faith and trust that I will be taken care of if I can't let go?

Time for another prayer asking to be shown how to surrender.

"Lorraine, your mammogram showed a teeny bit of cancer returning."

Sigh…

So, taking a breath and stepping back into gratitude, I was shown that I was still holding onto guilt and anger towards myself.

I was guided to suspend taking any medical actions or further testing for three months while I focused on my inner healing with all of my gifts and resources.

Standing in faith and trust with a medical diagnosis like cancer and not doing *what you are supposed to do* was very uncomfortable. I vacillated between peace and trust in what I was doing and feeling irresponsible for my health. The idea of getting cut again was upsetting.

So, I requested a follow-up mammogram to see if anything had changed and I was open to go through with a second surgery if needed.

Guess what happened?

The cancer cells they saw three months earlier were gone. A six-month follow-up was recommended.

Are you still with me dear reader?

We are living in incredible times. Awakening to who you really are is the journey *home* to reunite with your true self and Divinity.

Health issues, money problems, relationships falling apart, spiritual crises, all provide opportunities to encounter yourself at a deeper level as veils of illusion and pain fall away.

The path to freedom can be one of Grace and ease or one of pain and suffering. How much you surrender and embrace or struggle and fight will determine how easy or hard your journey will be. There were many times when I felt like I was walking through fire to clear and cleanse both myself and the world of pain.

You chose to be part of ushering in a new age and helping to reshape a new world. To do that, you must let go of what is no longer serving you to make space for what is ready to be birthed within you and *out there*.

I remember reading something Neale Donald Walsch wrote in his *Conversations with God* about the perfection in how the events in his life had unfolded and how much darkness had seeped into his life. He said to God, *"Yes God, I understand, but why do I have to deal with so much darkness?"*

God said, *"It depends on how much of a master you want to be. The higher the level of mastery you call forth, the greater the challenges."*

Oy vey! What did I sign up for?

The Truth Will Set You Free

"True freedom and the end of suffering are living in such a way as if you had completely chosen whatever you feel or experience at this moment. This inner alignment with Now is the end of suffering. Is suffering really necessary? Yes and no.

If you had not suffered as you have, there would be no depth to you as a human being, no humility, no compassion. You would not be reading this now. Suffering cracks open the shell of ego, and then comes a point when it has served its purpose.

Suffering is necessary until you realize it is unnecessary."
~ Eckhart Tolle

As miracles, blessings, and shifts continued to flow, I felt an excitement of being prepared for major work to be shared with the world. And the next level of clearing emerged with an intensity that brought me to my knees and everything went dark.

Over several weeks, my right arm became swollen with pain, I was in bed for almost a week with flu-like symptoms, and my left jaw cracked – hard.

It was time to face, feel, and let go of what I had been holding onto. My body was ready to purge.

It was time to get raw and deal with my feelings of rage, hurt, abandonment, betrayal, hopelessness, helplessness and distrust towards God. It was our day of reckoning.

"I hate you... I don't trust you... You are not my friend and we are not ok."

I let it rip. I screamed at God until I was sobbing. The grief was so deep…

I know there was nothing I said or felt that was unknown to God. I had never verbalized or allowed myself to feel the depth of my despair and pain. I watched myself as I sat in my victim and felt no solace or hope. I could not, would not let God help me.

I was no stranger to the darkness and this time the separation I felt with God was excruciating.

How can I live and do the transformational work with clients that I was born to do without God?

I cannot live like this anymore.

My close friends held me in love and support for whatever was next.

I'm a powerful manifester and I knew that if I continued to feel unhappiness and suffering that I would likely create a dis-ease that would take my life or I would commit suicide.

I've never been suicidal but when life is so deeply painful I can understand how contemplating suicide provides relief to suffering, whether a plan is acted upon or not.

I've had many clients in unbearable emotional pain who could not see a way out or through to find their way back into Light.

I watched my mother's unhappiness manifest leukemia and a dear friend created cancer as a way to leave this Earth life.

I have to surrender. I'm too exhausted to fight anymore.

Maybe I am complete and it is time for me to go?

Hell no, I'm not leaving! I've come too far and it's my time to receive the goodness that is mine, so make it happen, God!

One of my favorite metaphors is the Phoenix rising.

The darkness lifted and the Light rushed in.

"Are you with me God?"

"Yes child. I am with you always and forever."

On April 18, 2014 one week before my birthday, I received a clean mammogram report. I recall sitting anxiously in the waiting room for the radiology result and the wave of joy and gratitude when she handed me the report and said, "See you in a year." I thanked and praised God all the way home after a quick stop at Trader Joe's.

Had I not followed my heart, I would have had an unnecessary surgery and maybe worse…

I am learning the keys to surrender and flow with Life in ways I never have before. And the separation I felt with God is healing.

Transformation Is a Process, Not a Technique

"Life will give you whatever experience is most helpful for the evolution of your consciousness. How do you know this is the experience you need? Because this is the experience you are having at the moment."
~ Eckhart Tolle

Moving into higher states of consciousness invites you to see the world through different eyes. I often feel like being a stranger in a strange land learning a new language.

There is a vast difference between intellectualizing a concept and thinking you understand what something is and feels like and embodying the essence of what it means to KNOW and FEEL trust, faith, forgiveness and even love in your heart and soul.

To be fully alive you must fully feel every thought and emotion so they can be released without the effort of trying to control, direct, or manage what's happening in order to get rid of them as fast as possible! Efforting creates resistance.

Imagine a fire burning. If you continue to throw logs on the fire, it will continue to burn. If you do nothing, the fire will burn out. That's how you release without stuffing pain back into your body, mind, and soul.

Learning how to stay with the feeling without getting stuck in the story of what happened is the key.

How do you do this?

Below is a process I created that I guide my clients to master. I have included some insights from Michelle Mayur that enrich its power.

The Grace Release Process

Permanently releasing inner pain requires the willingness and courage to fully feel your emotions without attempting to manage, control, or direct the process with deliberate effort to *get rid of and rush through* letting go. This powerful process is not a technique. It is a turnkey approach to being fully alive without resisting yourself or life, moment to moment.

Use this process to work with any painful negative emotional charges. I will use several words interchangeably to mean God.

1. Become aware of what is happening. Notice body sensations, emotional reaction, physical pain that might be an emotional charge.
2. Breathe into the feeling that might be a recognizable emotion. You may not be able to identify or label what you are feeling and that is ok. It is all energy! I often say, "Give me more," to invite the energy to build for the most complete release.
3. Let go of the story, of needing to label and understand what you are feeling and why.
4. Put your attention several feet above your head to invite a connection with your Personal Divine (or whatever name you use to mean Divinity: Higher Self, Jesus, Buddha, Higher Consciousness, the Creator…). Imagine a column of Golden Light flowing down from your Higher Self and connecting with the top of your head. Breathe into that connection.

   Hold that intention, even if you don't sense or feel the energy with the Divine. Ask the Divine Presence to move down the column of Light and fill your body with its consciousness and to rest in your heart.

5. Continue to breathe and invite whatever you are feeling to intensify and **do NOTHING**. Clear your mind, let go of engaging in any way to direct, control, or manage what you are feeling! *Anything you DO, any effort you deliberately direct to try to help will create resistance and block the clearing.*

6. Feel and observe what is happening within you.

7. Stay with the energy and keep breathing.

8. When you have FULLY felt the energy or emotion, or believe you have, which may be several minutes or LONGER, ask the Divine to take it from you. I once released deep waves of despair for over 90 minutes.

9. Observe this release happening in whatever way you see or sense it.

10. As you let go, feel yourself standing in the Presence and in your power. Use your breath to deepen this connection.
    Stand up and say out loud:
    "I am the Power and Presence of God.
    I feel my Power coming back to me.
    I feel my power surging through me.
    I feel Divine Love flowing through me and as me."

11. Feel the connection strengthen with the Divine to allow Grace and peace to come in. Use your breath to deepen this connection.

12. With gratitude, rest into the energies of the Divine.

13. Breathe into the connection with the Divine and stay there as long as you like.

Remember that you are an energy being. Pain charges can come up in obvious or subtle ways, like a panic attack or emotional eating.

You might wake up with physical pain that might actually be an energy charge trying to be released from your body. How to know? Ask your Divine. Then work with this Grace Release process.

Understand that emotional charges can build up in the body like internal structures. The releases you experience can be the beginning or further dismantling of the structures you have been holding within you for a long time and may have been passed down through your ancestry.

Negative charges will continue to come up for release throughout your life. Welcome them when they show up, without anger and judgment, to allow them to clear quickly and with Grace.

Have patience with your process and your journey.

Charges may come up when you are unable to be fully present to use this process. Invite your Divine to help you hold steady until you can reconnect with your charge at another time.

The most important relationship to foster and grow is the one with the Divine. I have used *Your Personal Divine* in this process because your relationship with the Presence is personal.

This process becomes automatic and flows into each step. Play with this process and see what happens. Allow your Personal Divine to add or adapt this in ways that are right for you.

Don't worry about doing it perfectly. Your intention and willingness to stay with the charge with the Divine is the most important key to the process.

Follow Your Heart. It Knows the Way Home

"Life's weather is but temporary.
It's the seasons that really matter.
Finding balance in the storm. Life."
~ Anonymous

Everyone's path is different.

You may not always feel prepared for the challenges in your life and I believe the difficulties we face come in the forms that give us the strongest opportunity to create a shift and wake up.

As events in our world accelerate, and transformation occurs with more speed and gusto, it's critical to always be working on solidifying your internal foundation. Creating a solid inner foundation in harmony with your True Self, maintaining spiritual practices that keep you connected to your center of Divinity, and having activities that nourish you, will provide a *structure* to sustain the *earthquakes of life* to turn trials in triumphs.

You are not meant to travel your journey alone. Give yourself permission to ask for help from trusted friends, colleagues, coaches, gifted healers and those in the spiritual realms, to bring Love, Light, and Grace, so that you can weather life's storms with courage, faith, and trust. Help can come from expected and unexpected places when you are open to receive.

The spiritual journey is not an easy one to travel. The path can be terrifying and painful, exhilarating, liberating, empowering and humbling. ***Those experiences can be the most powerful gifts to your growth and evolution because they provide the greatest opportunities for healing and transformation.***

Trust and follow your soul's guidance. It knows the way home.

Learning how to let go of resistance to surrender and embrace each experience as a blessing brings the hand of Grace.

Breakdowns open the heart to Love. Self-Love unlocks the door to reunite with your True Self. Love is the key to awakening and creating Heaven on Earth.

Darkness is always a prelude to light.

I've often asked that if I knew then what I know now about myself and my life, would I have said, "Yes!" or hit the ground running?

I hope I would have said "Yes."

I'm grateful for the way things unfolded, one step at a time. Nothing was wasted. Every experience has contributed to my life. The same is true for you.

Bless everyone and everything. Experiences are meant to develop not envelop you! All has been in service to your healing, growth, and evolution.

In closing, I would like to say thank you for reading my story.

I believe that now more than ever, the real life experiences we share that represent triumphs bring hope and courage to boldly go where you have never dared to go before to live an awake, abundant, and meaningful life.

And thank you for making your transformation and spiritual path a priority that also benefits the world.

You are loved more than you know – and you never, ever walk alone.

This favorite quote has helped me to stay in courage, faith, and trust:

> *"When we come to the edge of all the light we have*
> *And must take a step into the darkness of the unknown*
> *We must believe one of two things*
> *Either we will find something firm to stand on*
> *Or, we will be taught to fly."*
> ~ *Patrick Overton, The Leaning Tree*

In One Love,
Lorraine

REV. LORRAINE COHEN (United States) is internationally recognized for one heart coaching, inner grace healing and higher light channeling. A fierce advocate for her clients' transformation, she uses her spiritual, intuitive, and healing gifts to support women to dive deeply into self–love, transmute emotional wounds and strengthen their personal connection to God to create a bold, abundant, and meaningful life. She is an international best-selling co-author, Unwavering Strength, Vol. 2 and writes for BellaMia Magazine. WWW.LORRAINECOHEN.COM

LORRAINE'S FREE GIFT: Creating a Magical Life Power Tools at HTTP://EMBRACEDBYTHEDIVINE.COM/GET-YOUR-BONUS-GIFTS/

The Best "Worst Time" of My Life

– Christine Kloser

God sure has a funny way of working in our lives. Being a coach for years and the author of *The Freedom Formula: How to Put Soul in Your Business and Money in Your Bank*, one of my core teachings was the Universe is always conspiring for your highest good. Yet it wasn't until I was put to the test in 2010 and 2011 that I discovered I barely knew what that really meant.

Let me share some background as I guide you through the greatest faith walk of my life. This is a story that I hope will help you see that even the darkest times of your life are filled with an abundance of light, and the unfolding of a glorious mystery that can deliver blessings and miracles that far exceed your greatest dreams.

An entrepreneur since 1991, I finally hit what most would consider the "jackpot" in January 2009: a successful coaching business, lots of new clients eager to work with me, a best-selling book, and generating nearly half a million dollars in revenue in a single weekend during a seminar I hosted in Los Angeles. I also co-owned a company that trained non-fiction authors to write, publish, and market their books, and I had manifested the perfect business partner to help me with that business, which I'd started back in 2004. Life was good as I sailed off to the Caribbean to celebrate my success with my husband and daughter. A picture perfect life, indeed. Or was it?

Let's see. That half million dollars of seminar revenue cost nearly $150,000 to produce. I ended up with $100,000 in uncollectible credit card charges as the credit crunch hit everyone hard, including many of my clients. I had paid far more than my budget could reasonably afford to hire high-level coaches to help me reach that goal, and my credit cards bills were proof of how much I had overleveraged myself in hopes of being a big "success."

To everyone on the outside, it looked like I had succeeded. But what kind of success was it when I had put everything on the line to create a business I *thought* I should have … doing what so many other coaches helped people do, namely make more money? Once I got honest with myself, I saw the truth that helping other people make money was not a passion that truly inspired me.

Transforming people's lives was my real driving force. Returning people to the magnificent truth of who they really are was my gift. Helping people reclaim and shine their brightest lights in the world was my unique blessing.

But, I had stepped away from this truth because I didn't trust it was "enough" to make a great living. ("Not enough" was a theme I was all too familiar with, being a high-achieving performer my whole life as a cover to make up for the deep-seated belief that I was never going to be "enough.")

Hindsight is always 20/20

Well, little did I know that stepping away from my deepest passion would be the very thing that would lead me down the path of financial ruin; an experience that terrified me more than anything. Wasn't money the only measure of success that really mattered? It was in the world I grew up in and, in my mind, financial ruin was the worst possible thing that could ever happen to a person.

Who was I, if not a financial success? What a powerful question!

So, after months of going through the mental, spiritual, financial, and personal anguish of realizing I had to stop doing what I was doing – and face having to file for bankruptcy, I felt my life was nearly over. How could I ever succeed again? Who would want to listen to what I had to say? I felt I was a supreme "failure." Maybe I should give up my dreams? How much worse could it get?

Well, maybe not that much worse because I still had a business partner and my small publishing company. That was the only shred of hope I had to get me through those very dark days. I knew I could double our revenues in 2011 and get myself and my family back on our feet. Thank you, God, for saving this one asset in all that we were going through!

Wait! What is this? A FedEx package the day before I'm going in to sign my bankruptcy papers? It's from my business partner's attorney saying she wants to buy me out of the company for a fraction of what it was worth. What? That was the only bit of stability that remained in my life. Even my marriage was on rocky terrain after all we'd gone through. If I didn't have that company, I had *nothing*.

This unexpected news (after months of planning with our attorney to protect the publishing company through the bankruptcy) impacted me more deeply than having my second pregnancy end in a miscarriage. It knocked me to my knees with a force that threw me down into darkness, pain, betrayal, and fear I'd never experienced before.

There were many days I thought I'd be better off giving up and crawling under a rock for the rest of my life. There were days I sobbed without end. There were days when I couldn't recognize myself through the rage that coursed through my veins. There were times when I felt like a monster for having the thoughts I had.

There were days I hated God. And, then there were many more days when I prayed for God to remove the hate and fear from my heart.

They were the worst days of my life.

And, they were the best days of my life.

A Walk of Faith

In the depth of that darkness when it appeared I had "nothing" left, I discovered that I had **everything** if I had my faith and trusted that the Universe really WAS conspiring for my highest good all the time!

(Remember, I'd taught this stuff for years, but was only now being asked to really LIVE it.)

Through the mess, the fear and the pain, a healing and transformation happened that feels like a miracle to me. Thankfully, just a few weeks prior to getting that FedEx letter from my former partner's attorney, I had begun to meditate.

I had struggled for years with a disciplined meditation practice. I just couldn't sit down and do it. But through a training I took in November 2010 in my hometown of York, Pennsylvania, I was inspired to meditate!

For the three weeks leading up to receiving that letter, I had been in conscious silence for an average of two hours a day, every day. I would wake up at 5 a.m. so I could meditate before my daughter would start stirring around 7 a.m. for school.

I also enjoyed taking time almost daily to do an ancient chakra balancing technique. And, I often found myself singing Sanskrit chants – celebrating the Divine – throughout the day.

These practices were a lifeline for me during this time of transformation. They enabled me to experience the magnificent peace and presence of the Divine even though I was losing my home, going through bankruptcy and trying to keep my business from my former partner. Through all of that "mess," I relished in the silence, and the song. I was comforted by the connection with the Divine I felt in my heart. I was able to release the pain, open to grace, and trust the unfolding that was underway.

These practices brought me an inner strength and trust I'd never experienced before. I could feel how much the Universe truly was conspiring for my highest good, and I was in awe of it all.

So, with this new awareness and trust, on January 20, 2011, I surrendered my personal will and leaped into trusting God fully when I stopped fighting to try to keep my publishing company, and sold my shares to my partner for a fee that didn't even cover my attorney's bill. It was the scariest and most liberating thing I've ever done! I'd never exercised faith like that before. I felt like I was on a wild adventure – with God at the helm!

Letting go of that company meant I had no known source of income; no concrete business at all. I had to rely completely on the Divine to help me navigate the new and unknown terrain of my life, and whatever new business was trying to emerge through me. I found an inner strength, confidence, and wisdom I'd never known before, and I promised God that I would use this experience in the highest service to others.

And, that's exactly what I did. Within weeks of signing the final papers with my former business partner (and also our final bankruptcy papers), it was clear exactly what I was being prepared to do! I had been guided every step of the way and received more miracles and blessings than I can count, which led me to launch a new business that was totally aligned with my unique gifts and blessings.

My new co-creation (this time around, my business partner was and continues to be God) is in service to visionary leaders who want to share their transformational stories through the power of the written word ... their books! This business is my bliss.

By the grace of God, I get to channel all of my passion for helping others heal, transform, and shine (ultimately for the purpose of helping all of humanity heal, transform, and shine). And I now combine these blessings with my practical know-how of what it takes to write, publish, and market a book. Calling this new evolution of my work a *match made in heaven* is an understatement. For me, this felt like nothing short of a miracle that had been in the making for years, if not lifetimes.

There is an abundance of evidence of that miracle in my life. I have since published three books featuring 80 amazing clients, plus some well-known #1 *New York Times* best-selling authors; I've created three new programs that have served upwards of 55,000 people in the three years since I went through this transformation; I bought an amazing home before I ever "should" have been able to, given my previous foreclosure; and more.

For me, this evidence is a sign of the incredible gifts that await us when we surrender to a higher purpose and do what we are truly here to do (with God by our side). I never dreamed my business could be this good, this joyous, this blissful, this rewarding, this impactful, and this abundant!

Let this book in your hands right now (and all of the powerful stories in it) be a sign of grace in your life. Open yourself up to seeing the miracles on the pages. Believe that no matter what challenge you are facing right now, you can transform through it into a whole new experience of yourself.

Namaste.

CHRISTINE KLOSER (UNITED STATES) is known as The Transformation Catalyst, and is a spiritual guide, award-winning author, and transformational book coach whose spot-on guidance transforms the lives of visionary entrepreneurs and authors around the world. Her coaching and training programs have impacted more than 55,000 authors to help them unleash their authentic voice and share their message on the pages of a book www. CHRISTINEKLOSER.COM

 CHRISTINE'S FREE GIFT: Free Audio Training for Budding Authors at HTTP://EMBRACEDBYTHEDIVINE.COM/GET-YOUR-BONUS-GIFTS/

If I Had Only Known Then What I Know Now

– Jesse Ann Nichols George

How many times could we say that phrase in our life? How often could we look back and wonder how different our life would have been if we had made different decisions?

I think if we are being honest, most of us could say that we have done this reflection many times in our lives. Some like to really beat themselves up over it. While some wouldn't change a thing, others think about how they may have had some amazing life if they had chosen differently; yet we don't truly know that either. We could literally "what if" things until the day we die if we wanted to, but truly what good would that do?

There is no question that I have made my fair share of poor choices along the way. Yet there is nothing quite like having intense life experiences to show you that there is no real point in worrying about what might have, could have, and should have been. Oh, yes, I spent time chasing after friends, boys, money, and all the so-called "good things" in life. Like many people, I was raised to make something of myself, get an education, get a good job, get married, to make a life.

After all, it is what you "should" do, that is the pattern for the way life is supposed to go. However, somewhere I always had a little voice deep within that said, "That's not you, that's not your life." Perhaps if I had known then better how to follow that little voice ... hmmm, who knows where I would have landed? Trust me, I listen a lot more now.

The time in my life that I am sharing with you here today has to do with the here and now. You might even be thinking, "Oh yes, I know all about living in the moment." Yet keep in mind that even though these concepts have been around for a long time, they haven't always been as accessible, on a public level, as they are now. So let me share with you my story on this.

I had been having some real physical challenges near the end of my time living on the Central Coast of California. At that time, I was in an HMO (Health Maintenance Organization) medical system, and I was still programmed with the mentality that when something is not right, go see a doctor. The doctor ran some tests and found that something was a little off with my gallbladder; however, it was not "far enough" out of the normal range. Forget the fact that I normally, most of my life, ran with perfect health stats. They dismissed me and sent me on my way.

Little did I know what was really going on with me. That little voice within was saying, "That isn't right, you need to pay attention to this." But the logical mind said, "Certainly the doctors know what they are talking about," and so I hung my head and went on. This was just the tip of several stressors in my life at the time, so I went off to just "deal with it" as best I could.

A few years later, still writing things off to stress and "bad luck," my body went through some bigger challenges. I would wake up and it would take me two to three hours just to get out of bed, as I could not feel my legs, nor could I see past the end of my bed. It was getting worse, and sometimes when I would go out to the store, my vision would get a little "funky" on me. Fear was starting to set in. What was happening? What was wrong with me? I was scared to drive because I didn't know if my vision would go while out in the car. Whose life besides my own might I take if this happened?

So more tests were run – apparently nothing was wrong with me, they said. Must be all in my head, they said. Again, I wrote it off as maybe I am just too stressed; after all, life wasn't great, working was a problem, and I was feeling a little lost in life. Then, there went that little voice again, "Something is wrong; you need to take care of it." Only this time, I thought, perhaps I need to start doing my own research on what was happening.

As I did this, I came right down to seeing I was dealing with what seemed to be lapsing/re-lapsing multiple sclerosis. So, I thought, "Great, how do I 'fix' it?" My heart was sinking as I read on about challenging lives in wheelchairs and drugs that were worse than the disease. Not to mention that they have to tap spinal fluid to test for it, which involves another set of risks.

Now what were my options? I went to a couple of support group meetings. Great people, most keeping a pretty optimistic outlook. Yet, it still came down to what was I going to do? What was right for me?

After pondering everything, I thought, "Well I have done a lot of healing for others and now it must be time for me." I could hear the bell tapping, as in, "Wow, what do you know, she might actually 'get it.'" I opted to stay away from the test for verification for MS; after all there wasn't anything they could do for me and I wasn't going down the route of meds from what I had seen and heard from people in the group. I at least had hope that I might get "lucky" and not deal much with it.

During all of this happening, I had a business that had failed, the man, whom I thought was love of my life, married someone else, and everything seemed to be crashing down at once. I thought, "I have all this knowledge and wisdom with Astrology and things, perhaps I should find my 'alignment spot' and move there. Wherever that is, I am going there." After all what did I have to lose? I had to give things every chance that I could.

I have to say that the great Divine has a real sense of humor because, thanks to finding my "alignment spot," it dropped me flat in the middle of the desert in Arizona. Right where I never wanted to live. Although, I didn't want to give up and face a life in a wheelchair, either. So, I packed up and moved. I took a job that I didn't have to think about, that I could walk away from at the end of my shift; and just focus on me. Little did I know that my earlier experience of being self-employed was meant to teach me, from what appeared to be failures, that my angels were trying to get me to learn how to succeed, that they were letting me know back then that I wasn't supposed to be working for someone else.

So, I made the changes, and thought all was improving nicely. Perhaps, I was right by finding this place. Perhaps, I just needed some dry heat to help me heal. Things seemed to be settling down as I took this simpler approach to life, or so I thought.

Some time went on, and I started noticing a few odd pains coming up in my body. I tried to be "tough" for a while with them, until they started to interfere with my work and ability to function. Now in the meantime, I had already been diagnosed with hypothyroidism and put on very high doses of Synthroid and Cytomel. I was also starting to have issues with breathing. This led to being diagnosed as insulin resistant and finding that I had Systemic Lupus Erythematosus – a form of lupus. Surely that must be why my body was swelling and starting to gain weight right?

I felt this was a gynecological problem, based on how and where the pain was hitting in my body, so I eventually went to a doctor. The breathing issues subsided, by the way, once I discovered through my own research that I was gluten intolerant. The doctor said, "Well I see a little something on your ovaries, but it is nothing to worry about." Again, trusting my doctor instead of my own body, I said to myself, "Oh ok, it must be the stress I am under again."

However, the pain never went away and got worse. The doctor eventually re-ran the test about a year later and said, "Well it has grown about three times in size, but it is so small we don't need to worry about it." There went the voices again, "WHAT!!!? That is not true, something is wrong." Even my logical mind couldn't follow the doctor's reasoning anymore. So I started my pursuit to try to find out what was really wrong, and how to heal it.

I went to doctor after doctor, looking for someone who would believe me. After all, I have always had a high threshold for pain, and even when intensely severe, have learned how to use mind over matter to remain calm and not feel it as much. Basically, because I wasn't complaining enough, no one was taking me seriously.

Finally, I got another opinion from a fertility specialist. I knew that she would not try to do anything that didn't need to be done. She was highly sought-after and had interns who waited years to work with her. Yet, my head hung low when even she said things were small and questionable, but at least she agreed to do more tests and to watch things more closely.

She did, in further tests, come to find that there was a blockage in one of my fallopian tubes. An outpatient surgery was then scheduled to remove the fibroid and to check for some other things. Unfortunately, that didn't go as well as we would have liked. I couldn't come out of the anesthesia they gave me and had to be admitted overnight into the hospital. The surgery was around 6:30 a.m. and I wasn't coherent at all until about 8:00 p.m. – and even then not fully so.

There's nothing like knowing your soul just doesn't really want to be with your body. My soul, I could tell, was going through another period of debating whether it was going to stick around. There were times when my body was lifeless and I was looking down on it from above. My heart was sinking, my hope fading… All this and I still had just as much pain.

When the soul is indecisive whether it will stay or leave this existence it is common to go out of body during this time. When the body is under tremendous suffering the soul realizes this is not a natural state and seeks to disconnect from the body so that the pain does not go to the soul level. It then can make the decision from a clearer space as to what it really seeks to do.

Upon going in for a re-check, the doctor was saying she would prefer not to do a hysterectomy; however, she was concerned that there was more happening, as I was not feeling ANY better than before the surgery. It felt like things were just as intense, and getting more intense by the day. My consolation? I was told there was no sign of endometriosis. She finally suggested that I have a consultation with another doctor to see what he could come up with.

I was drained, exhausted, and struggling to survive, only I didn't know just how much at that point. I finally got myself into his office and he ordered up – surprise – more tests. For over a year now, my life had been one big test after another, yet no one seemed to have any answers.

Only this time, when I went back to discuss the results with the doctor, to my surprise he actually found something. Not just one thing, but multiple things. He said there were some adhesions in my stomach and proceeded to ask me about abuse and receiving blows to the belly. I said there was none, unless you count the battles I fight in my dreams.

He went on to tell me that my colon was knotted and kinked, and that my bowel and bladder were not positioned right. As if that wasn't enough, he said that my gallbladder was horrendous. He asked if I had any known gallbladder problems and I told him that about 11 years prior they had noticed something and said they wouldn't do anything about it, because it wasn't far enough out of the normal zone. Then I got the kicker.

He said to me, "I don't know who you are, but there must be a reason why you are still here, because there is no medical reason for you to be alive. You should have died years ago." I sat there in silence. I didn't know what to think or say. Not only had he found something, but multiple things, and better yet, had no reason for why I was alive. He went on, "I would like to operate on you now, but can't because of the recent outpatient surgery you just had. Here are a couple of my cards, keep them on you because if your gallbladder erupts, they will need to contact me for emergency surgery."

I left his office, dazed. Now what? Life was supposed to get better here. Now I don't know from moment to moment if I will be alive. There is no medical reason for me to be alive. What do you do with that piece of information? I had been living on borrowed time for 11 years. "Oh man, if I had only pursued things sooner and listened to my guides," I lamented.

The doctor doing the outpatient surgery decided to go ahead with a full hysterectomy. So, in September of 2003, I went in and had six or seven surgeries done by two specialists (both in the top ranks countrywide), over a 6½-hour period. My parents came and stayed with me, certain that I wasn't going to make it and preparing for the worst.

I remember coming out of the surgery and saying, "There is no more pain, I am all better now!" The pain from all the surgery was nothing compared to what I had been through. I was even up and walking that night.

The next morning, both doctors were in to see me. What did they tell me? "You were in bad, really, really bad shape. You had to have been in immense pain. I can't believe you were even walking around." I thought, "DUH, I have been trying to tell everyone for the last couple of years I wasn't doing well." They said they had no idea and oh, by the way, I was loaded with endometriosis, even though the outpatient surgery had showed there was none there. Also, the other surgeon said I had the worst adhesions and gallbladder he had ever seen in his entire medical career. They were hardening like beef jerky and all of my organs had gotten stuck together from them.

Well, needless to say, the next three days I had tons of interns brought to my bedside as the doctors talked about what happened with me and told them, "Now THIS is something you will probably never see in your medical career again, but it is good for you to be aware of." I was a living miracle. I actually ended up being released early because I was healing so rapidly.

There was one little concern – a test that was a follow up to the surgery, which made the technician think my gallbladder wasn't removed. Yep, that is right, I had either a second small gallbladder or I was already regenerating a new one. Later down the line, I began getting some symptoms again. They scanned me and found that I was, indeed, re-growing or developing a new gallbladder. It was peace of mind having this confirmed, even though the news was also unsettling.

As time went on, I continued to be more proactive in my health and well-being, as I had learned just how fragile life can be. I had learned that you never really know whether you are going to have another day in your life. I had been fighting for my life for years and years, and finally I was going to be able to get back to living. It took everything in me to keep doing the work the doctors weren't going to do.

I made many changes to diet and nutrients, and have continued this path. As I healed, I had less and less need for doctors. As I stand in my awareness now, I haven't seen a doctor in about five years.

Now, I work completely with nutrition to remain strong in body, mind, and spirit. I managed to first remove myself from all thyroid medication and from hormone replacement therapy. These are things that you are not supposed to be able to get off of and this needs to be done with extreme caution and follow-ups with a doctor. When I got sick, they tested things and yes, I actually was in check with my thyroid, pushing the edge, but reasonably in check.

Now, I don't even need supplements. I stay focused on *high-powered and nutrient food*. I keep listening to that inner voice as much as possible. Now, when it talks to me, I say, "Show me what and how," and it is done. Life has changed enormously over the years.

What is scary? If I knew then, what I know now, I might very well have avoided all of that surgery, the doctors, etc. The resources out there are enormous, way over what I had to work with. Use them, and listen intently to that inner voice. If you feel like you are being shuffled around, don't give up. At the very least, honor yourself with the care you need. Your body knows, your angels know, you know. Now all you have to do is to simply listen.

A Few Tips & Thoughts

When I found out that there was no reason for me to be alive, I thought of how everyone is always saying, "Get out the bucket list and start doing everything that you always wanted to do." However, what if you don't have the budget to go do those things? What if those options aren't available to you? I didn't have those kinds of resources, as nice as it might have seemed.

Instead I opted to appreciate each and every day. I said to myself, "How do I make today extraordinary? How do I make this moment incredible? What if I just learned to appreciate the moments without all the hoopla?"

So I did. I woke up every day realizing that if I can be the medical miracle that I am, then it is time to figure out what I really need to be doing in this world. It is time to care more.

I spent time reflecting on all the times of being greedy, selfish, unappreciative. I reflected on the people and situations I had known in my life. I looked back on this journey that I had taken. I realized what an incredible place it had brought me to, and that there was no need to change a thing.

Moving forward, I operated with love in my heart. I found forgiveness for every place I felt wronged. It all seemed so trivial now. As Tim McGraw's song goes, "I spoke a little softer, and loved a little deeper." My heart was opening and, for the first time in a long time, the angels and guides were silent because they were basking in my consciousness with smiles. They were enjoying the moment with me. My life was never going to be the same.

After many more challenges, I have learned that it is really all in how we deal with things. What will you do with any given moment? These challenges come up not to break us, but to help us get re-focused, to make us stop and listen, and to create balance.

What got me through, was realizing that I wasn't meant to suffer. My life was full of meaning and purpose and I just needed to connect with it, and that is a whole other journey. I took time to care for me, to create balance.

I took up yoga, which helped develop my consciousness. I spent time with people who helped me develop further into myself. I stopped worrying about everyone and everything else.

I don't promise you that the road will be easy, or pleasant, or always full of joy. However, if you are willing to see the journey all the way through and be open to what it has to teach you, then you too will learn to find peace within, even in the darkest, hardest, most challenging times. If you will learn and grow, release and find the cycle for you, then you will see the beauty in everything that happens.

I often times would not only take a yoga class, but do some poses late at night on my patio. It was quiet and peaceful, and the moon's glow was soothing. I took time to take pauses. I honored my thoughts, feelings, and longings. However, instead of impulsively going after them, I learned to understand them. Yes, that is where I learned my true power.

What I did varied. Sometimes it was learning and researching, sometimes just total silence, sometimes music, sometimes sharing with others, sometimes yoga, meditation or visualization. For me, there is no one way or tool. I adjust and blend what feels right in that day and in that moment.

JESSE ANN NICHOLS GEORGE (United States) is the author of four books, which are founded on the principles of compassion, and how to use it to bring joy to all areas of life. She created The Genesis Clearing Statement and The Compassion Tour. Jesse is a Code Interpretor with over 33 years of experience working with clients and assisting others with their life processes. She is a spiritual healer and Druidic practitioner from a family of spiritual healers and Druidic practitioners for more than 13 generations. She is an energy tuner, life/relationship/spiritual and wellness coach, and holistic and natural lifestyle advisor. Jesse is a speaker and also hosts her own radio show. www.jesseannnicholsgeorge1.com

 JESSE'S FREE GIFT: "Genesis Clearing Statement – Have the Life You Truly Desire" at HTTP://EMBRACEDBYTHEDIVINE.COM/GET-YOUR -BONUS-GIFTS/

In the Hands of Angels
– Rev. Sage Taylor Kingsley-Goddard

Do you believe in miracles?

I surely do. I have been blessed to experience miracles that have changed my life, saved my life, and even brought me lasting love with my Twin Flame soul mate. When we are graced and embraced by the Divine, we *know* that what happened to us was both magical and real. Whether other people believe us or not! Here are several of my many true miracle stories…

In 1991, I was diagnosed with sarcoidosis (aka sarcoid), a mysterious rare disease that ravages the body. I had stabbing pains with every breath. My chest X-ray looked like I had advanced emphysema.

Doctors said, "There's not much we can do," and suggested steroids and painkillers. They predicted I would die young and be in pain all my life.

Sarcoid is a progressive, incurable disease that moves around the body and causes blindness if it reaches the eyes. I was looking at a life of disability. Pain. Possible blindness. Then death.

Ironically, sarcoid usually afflicts middle-aged African-American men. I was a white woman. And 26 years old.

I came home, fell to my knees, cried and prayed: "God, there must be something better for me than this! I am only 26! PLEASE guide me to a miracle. I will do anything, just show me the way."

And I was told to pick up a local magazine with listings about holistic health. I closed my eyes and was "told" while turning the pages: "Turn, turn, turn, stop! Point!"

My fingers landed on an ad for Dr. Lam Kong's Acupuncture & Traditional Chinese Medicine, about which I knew exactly nothing at the time.

At my first visit, I didn't think Dr. Kong understood a word I said, his Chinese accent was so thick. I kept trying to tell him the disease was in my lungs, yet he put all the needles in just one of my EARS.

He also gave me customized Chinese herbs with bizarre-looking plant bits poking in all directions. I drank the tea and came back for session two, feeling only slightly better.

Then the miracle happened!

While I was lying on the table with needles in my ear, I had a vision of myself being the size of a baby, with purple hair, held lovingly by a large angel with a rainbow halo. I knew the angel was healing me.

I asked, "Who are you?"

The angel said, "Archangel Gabriel."

I felt embraced and cherished, held and loved beyond description. And in that moment, the sarcoid disappeared!

I have been in "spontaneous remission" now for more 25 years. X-rays confirmed my lungs were healthy and normal.

I know that the combination of powerful Divine Healing from Archangel Gabriel AND the "Earth Angel" healing of Dr. Lam Kong with Chinese medicine was the EXACT combination that God guided me to, for my healing miracle.

When I thanked Dr. Kong for healing me, he humbly said in his halting English, yet with great wisdom, "Actually ... I have two things to say. First, I not heal you. I just REMIND your body how to heal itself. Second thing to say, I think you my 71st sarcoid successful treatment. (Looking thoughtful) Or, maybe 72nd. I have to check records."

I heard later from two acupuncturists in Hawaii, that he is one of the BEST herbalists in the entire country.

Dr. Kong has no Internet presence, so if I had consciously tried to find the best acupuncturist, who had cured more than 70 people of this ravaging disease, I could not have done so. God and my angels sent me to exactly the right healer at the right time. And Archangel Gabriel raised Dr. Kong's healing to the level of a bona fide miracle.

SO HERE'S WHAT I LEARNED FROM THIS EXPERIENCE:

1. *Miracles can happen in an instant.*
2. *God and our angels can heal anything!*
3. *Always follow my intuition and divine signs. (No matter how "out there" or illogical they may seem!)*

In 1994, the Divine embraced me again so powerfully it changed my life forever, and the lives of thousands of people I have been blessed to serve ever since … An unexpected shamanic initiation in the Mexican desert…

For a few months prior to the Day That Changed Everything, I'd been having strange death/rebirth dreams and was beginning to see colors, lights and sacred symbols and numbers clairvoyantly… (I wish someone had told me then, "You're not crazy, you're just psychic!")

It was a hot August day. I was visiting a friend in San Diego and we decided to go into Tijuana for some shopping, followed by overnight soaking at a hot springs resort in the Ensenada desert… You've heard the saying, "Man plans, God laughs?"

None of that happened. Instead, I had THREE Near Death Experiences (NDEs) – in 18 hours!

Each time my life was threatened, I was saved by divine intervention. A miracle! And by some means that I cannot explain, each NDE and miracle opened my Third Eye even more. I invite you to feel the power of just ONE of those three NDEs and miracles:

Going Through the Portal

Judy and I were sitting in my white Honda Civic, in line at the Mexican border. Suddenly I said, "Hey, look! On the other side of the border. Doesn't the ocean look like it's a different color?"

Judy replied, "You're right! Wow! It's bluer and deeper. How weird. Like it just suddenly changes right at the border line."

We stared at the shimmering water, incredulous.

Judy then exclaimed, "And look! The SKY is a different color, too! See, on this side how it's more polluted, darker and on the other side, it's clear and sparkly!"

"Wow! How can the sky and ocean change color at a border like this? Borders are artificial lines made by people. Whoa… This isn't just a border, Judy. I think we're about to go through a PORTAL."

I Just Wanna … Leave Tijuana

Upon arriving in Tijuana, we found it be a bustling city, filled with cars, people, stores, and vendors selling food from carts. We parked my car and set out.

Smells of car and bus exhaust mingled in our nostrils with the sweet scent of ripe mangoes and delectable aroma of tacos. Our simple goal was to shop, shop, shop. Judy wanted a poncho, I wanted a drum.

We ate lunch and were heading back to the car when I noticed an elderly Mexican lady, sitting in front of a store, with textiles and baskets before her. She was wearing a yellow blouse and purple skirt and was gazing right into my eyes, as if her entire BEING were smiling at me. I felt an infusion of energy into my heart and soul. My whole body tingled.

"Judy, did you see how that Mexican lady was looking at me? It's like she gave me some energy transmission or something…"

"Yes, that was mysterious. Well, who knows? Probably just a sweet old lady."

But when we turned the corner, still seeking the car, suddenly, there was the same lady! What?!

This went on for hours. No matter what corner we turned, we did *not* see my car but we *did* see the same old woman until finally Judy and I agreed she had to be a spirit or angel. No human could materialize in so many places at once. And each time the crone gazed at me, smiling, I felt my heart would burst.

We bought and ate The Most Delicious Mango in the Universe, sweet juice dripping down our chins, landing on our sweaty blistery feet in the 109-degree heat.

Refreshed by this nearly orgasmic mango experience, I said, "OK, we need to take a break and make a plan."

As we sat on a ledge and meditated, I was given a vision of a square spiral, opening outward. I opened my eyes and said, "Got it. We'll move outward in a spiral. We know we didn't cross any streets. So the only explanation is either a) The car moved or was stolen, or b) We're in an alternate reality. In either case, the car is not in the place it's supposed to be. But if it's anywhere in this city, if we go outward in a spiral, we will find it."

Judy thought this was brilliant, so around we went. One revolution … Two revolutions … And amazingly, we found the car. On Revolution #3.

On a street we had never been on before.

Carried on Wings of Love by the Angels

We collapsed into the car with relief and wonder. What Universe had we entered?

We caught our bewildered breath, then decided to travel south and find that desert hot springs we had heard about.

I was driving in the middle lane, when suddenly the red car to my left and brown car to my right both moved into my lane at the same moment.

And at that very instant, my car ROSE UP!

Hard to believe, and even harder to describe, but all I can say is that at the very second when the cars to the left and right both moved into the space where my car had been, my car was suddenly ABOVE THE WHOLE SCENE.

With me and Judy in it!

We gasped, looked down and SAW the cars almost hit each other right where our car had been a moment ago.

We were above the scene long enough to have this conversation:

ME: Where are we? How did we get up here?

JUDY: OH MY GOD!!! Those cars almost crashed into us!

ME: We're above everything!

JUDY: We would have been killed. How did this happen?!

Then, with no sense of descending, poof! We materialized on the road again, with the red and brown cars ahead of us, danger passed.

Judy's interpretation: "It felt like we were squeezed into a nothingness of space and time, compressed into a single dot and then suddenly not IN normal space or time at all. Outside the regular Universe."

MY INTERPRETATION: "That makes sense. I also FELT ANGELS' HANDS UNDER OUR CAR, raising us up until the danger had passed. An angel under each tire. Like we were floating on wings of light."

Thank you, Angels!

We wondered if one of us was right and if so, which one? How to understand the miraculous? We decided both of our understandings were equally valid, that we had experienced this Near–Death Experience and miracle in a way that made sense to us.

We learned that in the realm of Spirit, there are NO limitations.

And nothing is mutually exclusive.

And some people are actually angels!

Out of many perspectives, one truth can be made clear.

The other two Near Death Experiences that day involved a deadly scorpion, and a man trying to attack me through a car window. In both cases, a series of totally synchronistic things happened to save my life, including a three-legged dog, last seen 30 miles away, tripping my attacker. I believe this dog, too, was an angel, or guided by an angel.

As a result of the divine miracles I experienced during the most shamanic WOWerful 18 hours of my life, I went through a spiritual awakening. I was in awe to discover that my Third Eye and Inner Ear were blasted open and have remained open ever since. In 2008, I even became a channel for Archangel Michael.

Since that day, I see energy everywhere. I read people's auras and chakras, channel messages of Highest Truth and Love, and facilitate healing. Many of my clients tell me I am serving as the hands and voice of the angels. Yet I believe that *we are all here to be Earth Angels*. I am honored to be in sacred service and to witness many miracles, my own and those of the beautiful people I serve.

I also believe we ALL have intuitive abilities which are often squelched, and by Divine Grace, my own abilities were dramatically awakened.

It took me months after these three NDEs and angelic miracles to feel back in my body. I floated in an ecstatic state of love and felt zero fear.

Asking God for My Heart's Desire: My Soul Mate

Just as the Buddha learned that it is not enough to just sit beneath the Bodhi tree, and that we must live in the material world and engage meaningfully in relationships, or enlightenment is without purpose, I too have found that the application of spiritual connection and wisdom needs to be in the realm of relationship and right livelihood.

I'm a Pisces, which makes me a romantic. I'm also a Wolf Spirit, which means I have always longed to mate for life. Before I manifested my Divine Right Mate, I'd been through 20 relationships including divorce and two abusive boyfriends.

Here's how I went from the revolving door of Mr.-Not-Quite-Right heartaches, to the bliss of lasting soul mate love.

When I came home from that amazing experience in Mexico, I was able to realize (as Archangel Michael says, "Realize = See with My Real Eyes!") that I maintained a continuous comeUNION with Source.

So I asked God for the Number One Thing I Wanted Most: "God, can you please, PLEASE bring me my soul mate? I am so tired of being wrong and hurt. I so want to get it right this time!"

To which I got an answer that surprised me: "Yes. Pick up a pen."

I was puzzled. "No disrespect, but I don't see how a pen is going to bring me my soul mate. I would like you to deliver him TO me. Please?"

"Sage. If you are REALLY serious about manifesting your soul mate, you need to PICK UP A PEN. Now."

So I did. And 400 pages flowed out.

Here is part of what I wrote (from *The Radical Self-Love Guidebook*):

The Four Steps to Higher Love

1. **Love yourself. Unconditionally. Radically.**
2. **Heal yourself: Body Mind Heart & Soul. Turn your wounds into wisdom.**
3. **Clarify your heart's desires.**
4. **Manifest your mate!**

Sounds great, right? But HOW does one do all that?

The Good News God News is that I received dozens of specific practices for how to DO these four steps, and spent three years trying them.

I real-eyesed that I had been focusing on Step 4 (MANifesting!) without putting enough effort into Steps 1-3.

I wanted the Fast Forward Button. Get me to the Good Stuff! I don't want to do all this work, I just want my soul mate! NOW!

I learned that until we sufficiently do our INNER healing and alignment, our OUTER action fails to bring success. We just repeat unconscious patterns. Wash. Rinse. Repeat. Heartache #17. Ouch.

I had to learn to become my OWN soul mate.

Two of my mantras are:

"To find the love OF your life, first find the love IN your life."

"Don't settle for less, just to settle down!"

My Twin Flame arrived on Winter Solstice 1997.

A Dream Come True

I dreamed him into being. Literally.

One of the major areas of spirituality and healing I'd been researching and practicing intently since 1994 was sacred dreaming: using one's night dreams for healing and spiritual awakening.

Virtually every culture in the world has recognized dreams as gateways to the Divine. I began to teach shamanic dreaming workshops and retreats.

Ancient Egyptians, Greeks and Celts all practiced Dream Love Magic, to summon one's divine mate to appear in dreams. I practiced Dream Love Magic to ask for a dream of my Divine Soul Mate. You can try this yourself; feel free to reword it. However, keep in mind that to manifest successfully, you first need to do enough of Steps 1–3.

Fortunately you don't have to be 100% perfect or healed to attract higher love (hallelujah, right?); but you *do* need to heal most of your "baggage" – and energy field.

Anyone can appear to be a soul mate for the first six months thanks to brain chemicals including dopamine ("dope" a mine!), which can cloud judgment similar to drug addiction.

You have to deepen your self-love and make your intuitive radar SUPER STRONG so you use your "No" muscle and "Yes!" muscle appropriately.

So you can RISE in higher love instead of "falling" in love.

Dream Love Magic Prayer

Each night, just before falling asleep, I said this dream incubation prayer:

"Loving Spirit, please bring me a dream of my Divine Soul Mate. Let this dream take whatever form is for the highest good so we may find one another in this lifetime, if that is our best destiny. With Divine Timing, this or something better, for the Highest Good of All. Thank you!"

And soon I had this dream:

I was radiantly drifting through a shimmering cosmos when I see another glowing human form floating toward me. He is shining with love, with light. His smile fills me, makes my heart burst. I stop. I look at him, in awe.

I ask, "Are you the one?"

He replies, "Yes, and I will be with you in a few months."

He has blue eyes, dark hair, and a beard. I am magnetically attracted to him.

I fly into his arms, enveloped by his tenderness and wrapped in an infinite compassion that spans eternity. I embrace him with all of my being.

We are one.

I am home.

I opened my eyes, and then shut them – immediately! (Wouldn't you?) I wanted to stay in this bliss forever.

I knew this had been "more than just a dream."

I still felt filled with golden light. Boundless joy flooded from my heart. I knew that I had just reunited with my soul mate! And that he was coming to me soon!

Then my small mind-self kicked in, and I began to worry: How would we meet? What if I didn't recognize him? This was too wonderful to risk losing!

By closing my eyes, I kept the connection a little longer. I dashed out these questions to him urgently:

"Wait! Don't go yet! Tell me, how are we going to meet? How will I recognize you? What's your name? What do you do for work? I DON'T WANT TO BLOW THIS!!!"

He gave me an "it's-going-to-be-all-right" smile and reassured me: "My name is Mark. I'm going to answer your personals ad, and, as for work, well … I'm more of an artistic type."

I thought, "Oh no! Is he going to be broke or a mooch? No day job, an artist, hmmm…"

He must have "heard" my concerns because he said: "Don't worry, it will be all right. I'll see you soon!" And he was gone. But not completely because that dream kept our connection almost tangible.

I recorded all this in my journal and continued to float on Cloud Nine for months, knowing that soon I would touch my beloved again. I continued to follow Spirit's instructions, doing many deep practices of self-love, healing, clarity and manifestation until he arrived.

And just as he promised, Mark answered my personals ad three months later. He was a graphic designer then and is now a sacred Shamandala™ artist (shamanic mandalas).

True to his dream word, he never has been the type to wear a suit or have a day gag (my term for soul-sapping day jobs!).

That first moment when we laid eyes on each other in a Berkeley café, we declared at the same instant: "Oh my God! It's you again!!!" And burst into tears of joy!

And he was right.

It IS all right.

I was 99% sure he was The One, but here is another time I was embraced by the Divine regarding our love.

One day, while driving, I asked, "God, can you please give me a sign? I need it to be super clear because I'm only human and I can be pretty dense! I know you sent me the dream and it all FEELS right but I've been wrong soooo many times. I'd love another sign just to be sure. Is Mark the one for me?"

And at that moment, I heard a Voice say, "Turn on the radio." I heard/felt directed to change the channel … change … Stop!

"Can't find a better man! Can't find a better man!"

God, through Pearl Jam, confirmed to me that Mark is IT!

The last vestiges of fear, the wall around my heart fell away and we have been together ever since. Although we struggled financially at first, even experiencing the loss of our home and moving 20 times, our love and faith kept us strong. And by following Archangel Michael's channeled teachings, we healed our relationship with money and now enjoy a comfortable lifestyle. We recently bought our Dream Home and enjoyed a month in Europe. We are truly living our best, blessed lives and we love helping others do so as well.

To this day, we have a marriage so harmonious, we were recently featured in a book, *A Golden Love: Relationships of Divine Enchantment*, by Laura Dawn Bridges, MS & Craig Francis Nieuwenhuyse, PhD, as a "Golden Love couple" because we enjoy a romantic partnership so full of happiness, spirituality, and easy, joyous communication, that we embody divine relationship.

Important Things I Learned about Soul Mates

1. There are three kinds of soul mates: Karmic, Kindred Spirit, and Twin Flame. Everyone has many karmic and kindred spirits incarnated, but your one Twin Flame may/may not be incarnated. Your spiritual evolution helps you raise up the level of soul mate love you can manifest, and there is a right soul mate for you.
2. Of all my painful relationships, the one that hurt most was a soul mate but NOT a heart mate. Don't just ask for your soul mate. Ask for your Body, Mind, Heart AND Soul mate. And nurture your love on all these levels.
3. The deep self-love and healing, becoming your own soul mate, joyfully in love WITH LIFE, are the crucial prerequisites to lasting soul mate love. Mark and I don't just have a relationship. We have

an ELATION-ship, 18 years and glowing strong! My husband is an Earth Angel and being in his arms is being in the arms of an angel. And we know our angels guided us together.

4. I am delighted to tell you that not only will doing Advanced Law of Attraction practices via those four steps help you manifest your Divine Right Mate, they are also the keys to manifesting ANYTHING. (See below for manifestation re-SOURCEs that I am happy to gift to you.)

For me to go (and *glow*) from being divorced, bankrupt, disabled and struggling to being married to my Twin Flame, loving life, living in our Dream Home, thriving financially by doing what I love and making a huge positive global impact, I cannot give thanks enough to God, Goddess and my team of Angels and Ascended Masters. I have dedicated my entire life, my every breath, to serving God and Archangel Michael.

As you read these words, may they embrace and grace you with Spirit's Light and Love. May you always remember that you, too, are held in the arms of angels and that you are worthy, whole, holy and good. You are an Earth Angel yourself!

REV. SAGE TAYLOR KINGSLEY-GODDARD, CHT, RM, known as The Prosperous Goddess™, is a 6-figure Intuitive Abundance Acceleration Coach, Archangel Michael channel, shamanic Intuitive Miracle (I AM) healer, Reiki Master and Teacher, and a dynamic catalyst for personal and planetary transformation. Acclaimed author of *The Radical Self-Love Guidebook* and the creator of "Angelic Abundance Activator," voted #1 WORLD'S BEST LAW OF ATTRAC-TION PROGRAM, Sage passionately empowers heart-centered women to manifest more love & abundance! www.AngelicAbundanceActivator.com www.ProsperityPassionPurpose.com

SAGE'S FREE GIFT: Love Yourself Abundant Angelic Gift Set at HTTP://EMBRACEDBYTHEDIVINE.COM/GET-YOUR-BONUS-GIFTS/

Authenticity: Revealing the Real
– Rev. Edie Weinstein

*"We all have a face that we hide away forever and we take it out to show our-
selves when everyone is gone..."*
~ Billy Joel (The Stranger)

Each of us goes out into the world every day, wearing masks. We don them before we leave our homes, perhaps even before we arise from our beds. They serve as protection, subterfuge, entertainment, distraction and denial. Without them, we may feel naked and vulnerable and while wearing them, we may feel invincible. They evolved out of choices we made, some as far back as childhood.

We come into form as magnificent creations; tiny, fragile beings that radiate beauty, innocence and love. That is our true nature. As life has its way with us and we take on the fear-filled, limiting beliefs of the culture in which we are raised, our perception of our glory diminishes. Even the most confident-seeming among us have what I call *the monkey mind inner critic*, who yammers at us throughout the day, telling us that we are not now, nor will we ever be good enough, smart enough, attractive enough, rich, thin or successful enough. He/she is so sincere in attempting to persuade us that the lies spewed in our direction are the truth in the guise of protection that we put on a false face to convince the world of what we don't even believe ... that we are worthy of all we desire.

My mask looks like confidence incarnate as I am comfortable speaking with nearly any size group or only one person. It presents as Zen-like composure; a woman who rarely expresses anger. It shows up as the face of a caregiver who has used it as insurance that she will be loved. After all, who wouldn't be drawn to someone who meets their needs, sometimes even before they are expressed?

In recent years, I have been willing to peel away the façade and be truly seen for whom I am; a strong and vulnerable thriver who has been through challenge and change like every other being on the planet. Someone who is perfectly imperfect, Divinely Human and Humanly Divine. A woman who cries and laughs easily, who bonds quickly with kindred spirits.

I have become abundantly aware of how often I run the gamut from desiring to be seen, being embarrassed about wanting to be seen, to allowing – if ever so briefly – to be fully seen, to hiding again and then resenting that I'm not being seen. It can get exhausting!

To be witnessed and embraced for all that we are; the good, bad and ugly; as striving human beings, daring to reach for the stars, is a gift beyond measure. I like to say that I don't have the right to tell anyone what to believe spiritually and yet, my sense is that we are sparks of the Divine, dancing through the cosmos, being all fabulous.

For many of us, God is an enigma and wears different faces, some friendly and some frightening. What if, as the Joan Osborne song asks: "God was one of us?" How would that change the ways in which we view ourselves, our roles in the world and how we interact with the other "God-beings" that inhabit the planet with us?

Several years ago, I attended a Goddess Retreat that honored our Divine Feminine aspects. One of the activities was body casting and we could choose the parts we wanted to keep around for posterity. I had been at two others and in the previous years had cast "the girls," since they are among my favorite body parts, with one set more ornately decorated with flowers and hearts and the second one simple gold. On this particular occasion, I chose to do something I was more nervous about: covering my face with plaster and breathing through two little holes for about 20 minutes. As an artist and art teacher, the woman who wrapped me up knew what she was doing and patiently sat next to me, holding my hand, talking to me in a soothing voice, as I began hyperventilating, and then more calmly breathing through my anxiety. When the mask had hardened, she peeled it off and we set it aside to dry. A few hours later, I painted it, embellishing it with flowers, a heart over my third eye and throat chakras and finished it off with starry eyes.

At home, I mounted the mask on my bedroom wall and on it perched a hat I had gotten many years earlier and placed angel wings behind it. Quite cosmic, if you ask me, and also a wonderful metaphor for how I have lived most of my life. On the surface, things look pretty and shiny, colorful and fun, a glowing visage. Beneath the surface lie fear, hesitation, doubt, anger, resentment, insecurity and gulp … neediness. I have hidden it well, or so I thought. My M.O. has been to be the go-to person when it would serve me to be the get-to person who allows herself some real-ness, some BE-ing rather than busily doing so much of the time, more being cared for rather than only being the caregiver.

In March of 2013, I took a much delayed leap into a life-changing experience. For many years, a long-time friend had been inviting, beckoning, cajoling, tempting and otherwise convincing me to take a training called Woman Within International ®. An offshoot of what is called the ManKind Project ®, it creates safe space for women to dance with their demons and celebrate their delights. Having been a career therapist, my first thought was "I know this stuff." Janet sagely shook her head and reminded me that there was always more to learn and that I would likely emerge with more insight into what makes me tick. It was quite the hero's journey, or as I think of it, the s/hero's journey. There was a call to action and adventure, a dive into the cavernous depths that echoed with moans of my own fear-filled creation from eons ago – facing my dragons and emerging from the swirling waters, gasping for life-sustaining breath, bringing back armloads full of treasure that, more than a year later, still spill out before me.

Although over the years I have experienced loss layers of an ectopic pregnancy, the long-term illness and subsequent death of my husband with whom I shared a paradoxical marriage filled with caring and chaos, devotion and dysfunction, destruction of our house in Hurricane Andrew in Homestead, Florida in 1992, and being an "adult orphan," I still minimized my feelings, since I reasoned that other people had many more hardships and I prided myself on being a resilient thriver.

One of my intentions prior to registering was that I refrain from caregiving "savior behavior," a co-dependent need to fix, save, heal, cure, kissing all the boo boos and making them all better, as I learned all too adeptly from my well-intentioned parents. I was to be there as a participant and not a therapist, as tempting and pseudo-safe as that was. My experience has been that as soon as I commit to taking a workshop, it has already begun and the lessons come fast and furious. This was no exception.

The weekend was filled with opportunities to challenge my limiting thoughts and stretch my comfort zones; standing emotionally naked and vulnerable as I peeled off layers of protective armor that felt at times as if it was soldered on to my skin. It had also been an insurance policy against rejection. Unfortunately, those symbolic premiums were too high and the payoff not always sufficient to cover my needs. I often felt depleted and could feel resentment bubbling under the surface, like lava about to erupt. Each time it did, I pushed it back down in an attempt to cap it off, with a boulder-sized rationale that all would be fine, no matter what. While that might ultimately be so, by ignoring my feelings at the time, I was doing myself a disservice and forgetting that "What you resist, persists," according to Carl Jung.

The thing is, denial can masquerade as high functioning and no one would know what was bubbling under the surface. On that weekend, I experienced a cracking open of the shell that had encased my heart for as long as I can remember, but most recently reinforced by my mother's death in 2010. Tears melted the glaciated covering over the anahata (heart chakra) that had served as a sense of protection from the pain of the loss. I had erroneously believed that if I remained in the light, then the darkness of grief couldn't touch me. The same dynamic is true in relationships. On the surface, it appears that I am close to many people. The reality is, I have many people in my life; I am a magnet for loving souls who show up by overt or subtle invitation and I do treasure them *and yet*, it occurred to me that I rarely let people in deeply. I can name a handful who are permitted access to the inner sanctum and even they do not get to stay very long. It's the old belief of not wanting to take up too much time or inconvenience anyone. It also takes the form of keeping potential relationship partners at bay, since if I don't let anyone in fully, they can't leave. Sound reasoning, huh? So I dance for a brief time with whoever shows up and then we step away, leaving a piece of each other in (hopefully) safekeeping.

I spoke with two friends on the phone afterwards who told me the same thing; see I'm not as opaque as I might have thought, since they long ago saw through the façade. Both were glad that I showed up, rather than the mask, and that in their presence I was able to peel it back. I have to tell you that it was even more of a relief to do it metaphorically than it was to do it in actuality those few years ago. More tears and revelations occurred and one encouraged me to take baby steps in order to honor myself and my needs and the other was glad that I was really feeling, not going back into hiding as I was tempted to do. Afterwards, I felt all cried out with a softness that I have rarely permitted.

One of the benefits of doing this training is the ongoing support of what are called E-Circles (Empowerment Circles) of women who live nearby. I had the experience of my first one recently that consisted of four other women – three who have been in my life for durations ranging from 10 years all the way back to nearly 30 years, and one I met yesterday. All were committed to showing up fully for themselves and each other. Authenticity and integrity are hallmarks of these trainings and follow-up groups.

I came to the gathering with an intention to explore a longstanding issue. On December 21, I noted the 15th anniversary of my husband's death. I honor what Michael and I shared in the 12 years we were together, as we co-published *Visions Magazine* from 1988–1998, which seed-planted the crop that became my career as a journalist. I acknowledge the joys and sorrows, the pain and pleasure we experienced as perfectly imperfect soul mates who unpacked our baggage with each other, butted heads and blended hearts. Since then, I have had short-term relationships and (mostly) exquisite lovers (with a few "Oops, what the heck was I thinking?" men tossed into the mix), but have not met anyone with whom I could imagine sharing a life. I have been doing a great deal of inner work, figuring out what a healthy relationship could look like, since I have been on my own for so long. I wanted the group's guidance for sorting through the piles and stacks of stuff that were standing in the way of what I both craved and cowered to anticipate. I have an amazing life, filled with friends who are my treasures, unlimited creative outlets, extraordinary adventures and an attitude of gratitude that fuels it all. And yet, there is wistfulness, asking "What's wrong with this picture that I haven't yet found someone with whom I can share the wealth?"

As I began to speak, I noticed that my throat felt like it was closing up and my solar plexus seemed constricted. I asked the group to take a few deep breaths with me and let out a sigh/moan in unison. It was a freeing experience that allowed me to express what was on my mind and in my heart. My friend Janet, who has known me the longest, spoke up and pointed out, "I notice you use the word tap-dancing a lot." I often describe myself as, "Little Shirley Temple, tap-dancing for approval," a pattern that developed in childhood. She then asked me to put those words into action by literally tap-dancing while I continued talking about my feelings of being the caregiver in most of my relationships with men. I had a fear that no man was strong enough to support me emotionally. In very short order, I noticed myself getting winded and tired and my friends encouraged me to continue both tapping and speaking. I did that until the tears began to flow. They had asked me what else I wanted, in addition to this relationship. I told them I wanted to be center stage with my teaching work. When they wanted to know why, I told them it was so that I could use my gifts and talents and support myself while I was supporting others. The words "I want to be wanted for who I am and not for what I do," spilled out with my tears.

When I stopped dancing, I stood before each woman and repeated that statement and they, in turn, told me how valuable and loved I am without doing, simply being. Frightening statement, that – since my entrenched belief has been that if I didn't step into that go-to girl role, then who would want me? It was both my freedom and my bondage, a velvet rope that wrapped around my heart. I am unwinding it and taking off my tap shoes, retiring them in favor of soft, comfy slippers as I welcome a partner with whom I can play footsies.

In Heinlein's classic, *Stranger in a Strange Land*, the characters use the phrase, "Thou Art God," with all love, reverence and respect, and saw that God-spark in each other and within themselves. There is nothing blasphemous about recognizing the Divine in the person standing before you or the one whose eyes, sometimes blinking with disbelief, gaze back at you from your mirror. Perhaps that is one of the keys to the door we have kept locked, that has behind it all that we wish to draw into our lives.

What if your true colors could shine radiantly and you could completely live in the innocence of the newborn that you once were? How brilliantly would you radiate?

Self -revealing exercises:

MIRROR-MIRROR

Stand before a mirror, ideally full length if you are feeling particularly brave, and gaze at the woman whose image reflects back. Rather than using the glass to find fault, allow yourself to be fully seen. Smile at her, use the same loving words you would for someone you adore. Be aware of the emotions that arise.

WALK IN LIKE YOU OWN THE JOINT

My wise mother Selma used to share this guidance as a confidence builder. Head held high, eye contact, shoulders back and I add "knockers up!" Practice entering a room like you own it. Get your swagger on. Strut your stuff. The thing is that when you own the joint, you are responsible for its upkeep.

As My Own Woman

Make a list of your values and what you stand for; what I call a *wo-manifesto*. Some examples from mine:

I live full out, regardless of what anyone thinks.

I refuse to dim my light for anyone in order for them to feel comfortable.

I accept all the abundance that the Universe offers.

I forgive myself and others for perceived slights.

I live with compassion both inwardly and outwardly.

I see my own beauty, without the "Yes, buts," and "If onlys," simply … as is.

I move with grace, dancing to whatever music I hear.

I sing out with enthusiasm.

I speak my truth.

I welcome Love in all forms.

I refuse to second-guess myself.

I tell the people in my life what they mean to me.

I keep my heart open.

I imagine beyond limitations.

I mirror back the beauty in others I encounter.

I walk barefoot literally and figuratively.

I refrain from "guilty pleasures" and instead simply call them pleasures.

I ask for what I want, knowing that I may not receive exactly as I have asked.

I accept what is for the Highest Good.

I embellish my body with colors, fabrics, and designs that make me feel good.

I move on when a situation warrants it.

I sit with my own feelings, not pushing them away out of fear.

I surrender to what is.

I trust in Divine timing.

I unburden myself of excess baggage.

I live in integrity.

I am genuine and transparent; what you see is what you get.

I am learning to be subtle.

I say "yes" and "no" with equal ease.

I ask for what my work is worth without stuttering, and I expect to receive it.

I bungee-jump emotionally, enjoying the ride in free-fall.

I stand in my own Truth.

I breathe.

Rev. Edie Weinstein, MSW, LSW (United States) is a colorfully creative journalist, dynamic transformational speaker, licensed social worker, interfaith minister, radio host, bereavement specialist, addictions counselor, PR Goddess, Cosmic Concierge, BLISS (Brilliant Insightful Loving Safe Service) coach and the author of *The Bliss Mistress Guide to Transforming the Ordinary into the Extraordinary*. She refers to herself as an *opti-mystic* who views the world through the eyes of possibility. www.opti-mystical.com

Edie's Resource: www.vividlife.me It's All About Relationships radio show – Thursdays at 8 p.m. EST.

Pee Wee, My Kelpie Mate
– Linda Murray

Stepping out through the back screen door and onto the porch, another beautiful sky painted with streaks of reds and yellows greeted my eyes. Within seconds the sun smiled in a big golden glow to grace the morning summer sky.

Jostling each other to stand by my side were my three beautiful young Kelpies – Chi Chi, Miss Lily, and Yodi – alongside Pee Wee, their eight-year-old mother. Lucy the stumpy tail cattle dog made up number five.

Pulling on my boots, I headed down and let out the chooks, already lined up, ready and waiting for another day of free range foraging. Walking on to the feed shed I gave the dogs their usual handful of biscuits before mixing a couple of handfuls of lucerne, coconut and oaten chaff as the token gesture to bring the horses in for their visual health check. In their usual routine, the dogs ran on ahead sniffing the ground and checking out overnight stories as I walked along, the feed bins swinging in my hands.

Horses fed, and now satisfied all was well, the dogs raced back for a quick dip in the dam before racing on to beat me back to the feed shed.

Now back at the house, I sat on the steps to pull off my boots. Anxious barks from the dogs, inside the tractor shed, relayed the alarm. "There's a snake, there's a snake!" Yet, their message did not seem to be carrying the full *danger, danger* signal.

As I ran down to the shed, I was careful not to distract the attention of the dogs and perhaps have one bitten. On arrival and cautious investigation, I could see the tail and body of our resident diamond python, appearing out behind an unused pallet that was lying on the brown dirt floor. A multitude of thoughts flashed through my mind as I surveyed the scene, thank you heavens for no brown snake! Odd though, the thought flashed through my mind, "He's perfectly stationary, and why is he on the ground?" He usually is only ever seen in the rafters. "Why isn't he moving?"

With breath held, I carefully moved the pallet. Even though he was a python and not venomous, I felt nervous. Nothing! "Weird." I thought, "The python is partially inside the wood pallet structure and never moved. Maybe it's dead?" Tentatively I touched his beautifully patterned tail of yellow and black. Still no reaction! Yet there was life. Carefully I pulled the python backwards by its tail as I felt my heart thumping in my chest.

"Oh no!" I was shocked as his head finally emerged from the pallet. This beautiful creature had a bad head injury. Yet not an injury inflicted by the dogs. Very gently I covered the python over with a sturdy white fertilizer bag, to provide him some shelter. "What was the best thing to do now? What about some energy work? How could this python possibly survive these injuries?"

Hardly had I walked inside than the excited barks of the dogs could be heard once more. "Now what?" Sprinting outside and down to the shed once more, I could see a python outside the shed. "What's going on here, surely not another one?" Yet no, on closer inspection, Pee Wee had likely perceived the python as a threat to her (grown-up) children and in the way she had always protected them, dragged the danger out and away. So now my python had sustained extra injuries. I was devastated.

Pee Wee was called off and I told her the python was friend, rather than foe. Pee Wee was confused, she had been carrying out her maternal protection instincts.

The dogs came to heel on command, back up to the house we all walked. All the young dogs were tied up, now for Pee Wee. Pee Wee was never tied up these days, unless on the rare occasion she was in some sort of trouble. As I called her onto the veranda to be tied up at her comfort bed at the back door, she communicated confusion at what she had done wrong. Despite reassurance she was not in trouble, she remained unconvinced. She laid down looking very unhappy, her beautiful brown eyes tinged with sadness.

Next step, off I went back down to the shed, brown cardboard box big enough to contain our python, in my arms. Operation python rescue. As gently and carefully as possible, the python was placed inside the box and made comfortable. What a relief to close the lid, a python now totally safe and secure. Now placed in the shade of a magnificent wisteria tree, laden with cascading perfumed lilac flowers, the perfect place for our python friend to be!

The python passed over and I buried him in the garden, to lie at rest between a koala and a goanna.

"Righto Kelpies, time to run free again." As I reached down to unclip Pee Wee, her eyes met mine. I felt her heart connect and the word *poison* came to me. "What does that mean? Maybe she's saying she thought our python was a snake." I telepathically messaged her that she was forgiven, she was following her mothering instinct, I loved her and all was well.

Little did I know, this was the last time I would ever see her alive. The word poison would be revisited again and again.

The sun dropped down on the horizon, indicating evening feed time once more. Off we went to round up the chooks. No Pee Wee. "Maybe she's sulking up at her favorite log? Unusual, though, at this time of day." "Pee Wee, Pee Wee," I called and whistled. No answer and no dog. "Odd. Oh well, I'll see her later."

Feed bins tucked under my arms once more, the dogs raced ahead in their usual routine. With horses fed and feed bins stashed away, we all returned to the house. "Where's Pee Wee?" The word poison came back to me. "What did it mean?" Other Kelpies tied up and bones chewed, yet still no Pee Wee. Now I was really concerned. No amount of calling, or other Kelpies searching gave up any clue as to where she may be. Darkness fell. I brought out the torch to check all her favorite haunts ... not a thing. I felt so bad.

I began to have the feeling Pee Wee had passed over. Maybe she had gone away to pass over. It didn't make sense, Pee Wee was perfectly healthy. I felt so sure she was close by. She had never in her eight years left the property without permission.

Sleep eluded me. "What did she mean when she said poison? She hadn't been bitten by a snake." Kookaburras noisily chorused the dawn. I jumped out of bed, pulled on my slippers and ventured outside into the morning dew, full of hope. No Pee Wee. I was deflated. Dressed for the day I let the other dogs loose. With a little encouragement, they let out a chorus of healthy barks and howls. Despite my hopes, Pee Wee never appeared.

Although we were divorced, my ex-husband and I were good friends. He co-owned Pee Wee with me, and was away for the weekend. I texted that she was missing. No reply.

Feeding quickly done, it was time to search on horseback. The closest paddock beckoned me, especially as Pee Wee would bark if she were caught up. Plus her Kelpie mates would find her for sure without the noise of the bike. They were well skilled in getting results from the command, "Find!"

The extra height, from riding up high on my horse, provided another advantage compared to the bike. Two hours passed as we crisscrossed through the tall grasses and among the trees. Not a sign. Suddenly the dogs were very interested at the base of a big old gum tree. "Yes, Pee Wee!" I thought. I raced over to find an old koala had passed away and fallen out of his tree. That brought mixed reactions.

Picking the old koala up, I took him back and buried him alongside another of his mates in a back garden. Now back inside the house for a quick cold drink, I saw the text message ... no one was coming to help with the search. I was furious.

Since I had searched earlier, my anger and resentment had grown because I was searching on my own, when her co-owner was a mere few hours away. In my judgment, my mind ruled that, while I was only too happy to give up my weekend for my best mate, another was not willing to do the same. My mind told me my beloved Pee Wee had freely given more than 3,000 days of devoted loyalty and support, of dutifully watching the gate for visitors and strangers, of dedication in mustering cattle, and on snake watch, as well as being the wonderful caring mother of generations of great Kelpies. "So why would a person who continually told this dog she was a best mate, leave her in the lurch in her time of need?" The selfishness in refusing to give up less than 40 hours for a best mate, who had freely given more than 72,000 hours of devotion, was beyond my comprehension. My anger simmered and low frequency negative energies increased. My judgment overwhelmed the situation and blocked my ability to tap into myself to connect and ask for help to find Pee Wee. I was in no position to realize this at that time.

Now very angry, I swapped my horse for the quad bike, to search the far paddocks. My gut feeling told me the unlikelihood of Pee Wee being there. Bouncing and bumping over the rough ground, around big rocks and around the dams, my mood did not improve. No sign of Pee Wee having been anywhere.

"Ok, so neighbors next," I told myself. This, in spite of my feeling Pee Wee was close by. From neighbor to neighbor, not one person had seen or heard her.

Back home again and feeling very despondent. I was now even more certain in my feelings Pee Wee had passed over.

Sunday dawned as another beautiful, fine, sunny day, for a day of half-hearted searching. Not a sign of Pee Wee to be seen anywhere. "Where should I look?" Back I went to every hollow log and all other favorite places in the vain hope Pee Wee would miraculously appear. I felt so hopeless, tired and useless, as again I had nothing to show for my efforts.

That afternoon my ex-husband returned. I could hardly hold my anger and rage. I told him everything I felt. He was downcast and I felt remorse when he expressed his regret that he was the one who would live with his decision for the rest of his life.

Monday came with Pee Wee at the forefront of my mind. I had now realized my judgment blocked any assistance the Universe was giving.

My judgment, resentment and anger were all causing me to vibrate at lower and lower frequencies as my mind added fuel to the fire.

Who was I to judge other people's actions? Who was I to decide what was right or wrong in this or any situation?

As I released my need to control the mechanics of how I thought everything should be, results began to flow.

As I checked fences, with Kelpies in tow, for broken or twisted wires from kangaroos jumping through, or for branches over fences, so cattle may pass through, my mind ran to Pee Wee. Without any real expectation, as I rode along, I asked the heavens from the depth of my heart for a sign that would tell me whether Pee Wee was alive or dead. My instincts were she had passed over. I really needed to know, I couldn't bear the thought she may be being hurt and injured, all alone.

I clearly remembered from my childhood, when my dad's best sheep dog Rascal disappeared, in broad daylight, out of the blue. The dog I named as a puppy, so very special to me. Many searched high and low for Rascal. As time would tell, I was intuitively led to a small group of dead trees to find Rascal stuck by his collar, a mile or so from home. Rascal was alive and so overjoyed to see me. Although dehydrated and hungry, he recovered and went on to live to a ripe old age.

Back from the fence checking, I parked the quad in the shed. My attention was then drawn to a group of dusky gray Apostle birds, who noisily chattered and fluttered alongside the chook house. As I walked inquisitively in their direction, off they immediately flew, noisy chatter and all. They headed up to our country dirt road, toward two crows perched cawing in the old ghost gum tree up there. "Oh, look at those crows," I thought. "What have they got up there? I'll have to go and see."

Gingerly I picked my way through the many clumps of long green grass and carefully negotiated a path through the rusty barbed-wire fence, and now I was on the roadside. The Apostle birds excitedly squawked above me and the crows departed. Glancing around, I spied a pile of old brown glass beer bottles. "These bottles must have been there for 20 years or more and I had no idea," I thought to myself. I pondered why I had been brought to this place. "Let's ask the Apostle birds... What is there here for me to see?" I voiced aloud. The answer came in a chattering over to the right. I turned toward the chatter and looked down at the ground. Partly buried in the loose brown dirt were the remains of a brown leather shoe. Nearby, an untidy pile of rusted tin cans. "Where did this stuff come from?" I wondered. "I've lived here for years and never knew any of this was here," went my thoughts. Suddenly "What's this?" as I spied and picked up a little white jar. Almost perfectly clean, glistening white, an alabaster jar in perfect condition fitted snugly in the palm of my hand.

Immediately, thoughts flashed through my mind ... "White? White is peace. The jar looks like an empty urn." Immediately I knew for sure, Pee Wee had passed over and I was going to find her body. Pee Wee was at peace, and for now, so was I. "Thank you, Universe, thank you, thank you, thank you."

As I lovingly carried my precious jar home, I cried tears of sorrow as well as of gratitude. I had my answer.

"Where was Pee Wee?"

The following day I again rode the quad bike. This time I checked cows for new calves and fed them their booster feed. Without a conscious thought of Pee Wee in my head, I felt the distinct urge to return to where my search began. With hardly a hesitation, I turned around and headed the bike over that way.

As I stood and unlatched the gate, I once again received a prompt. The urge was to search more over to the left. Originally I had ridden more to the right and out to the trees. I slowly rode the bike to the left and gazed to the left, to the right and all around. I was hopeful and feeling a little optimistic, that this was the day. This feeling was especially so, with receiving the gift of my little white urn, from the day before. Within minutes there was Pee Wee, lying at peace in the paddock, her head pointed towards home a couple of hundred meters away (around 220 yards). I stood and looked down at her body. Her body seemed so small in death, when she was so large in life. As I stood there, my sadness and grief for her passing washed over me, and at the same time many wonderful memories of a dog so well loved and adored. With my head downcast, I returned home and gathered up a blanket for her burial. Once more back in the paddock I removed her collar as a mark of respect. Her working days were over, her duties complete. Pee Wee was running in total abandon once more, exactly the same way she came to this world.

I buried Pee Wee alongside her best mates and among animal friends. The hole took so long to dig, as so many tears flowed and blurred my vision. Finally I farewelled my friend, and with the last shovel of dirt completed, I placed a cherished piece of driftwood as her marker.

That night I told my ex-husband that Pee Wee was buried in the garden. He again expressed remorse and guilt for not returning to find his best mate. My heart again softened as I felt his sorrow.

These days I often wonder what Pee Wee thinks as she sees the flowers now blooming in all the colors of a rainbow all around her burial site.

The next day saw me out driving the tractor to help lift me up out of my despondency. Driving a car, riding the bike or driving the tractor, have always been avenues to allow the Universe to drop messages to me. As I drove around and around the paddock my thoughts were with Pee Wee. In the next moment I felt Pee Wee sitting under my seat and pushing up against my feet as she always did. She loved to ride in the tractor. She would sit on the ground outside the door and ask if she could jump up and in. No matter whether we were planting, ploughing, or mulching. No matter how hot we got in the cab if the air conditioner decided not to work, Pee Wee always stayed the distance. Even if that meant eight or 10 hours, with only a quick lunch break, Pee Wee was there, occasionally asking for a pat or a scratch around her ears.

Later an animal communicator told me in passing that animals tend to stay very close to us for a couple of weeks after they pass over, to help us with our grieving. I now believe this to be accurate, after I saw my old stallion a couple of days after he passed. After another horse passed, I had a little bird come into the house every day for a few days. The bird had never come in before and never again since.

After Pee Wee passed, I spent several days questioning if the outcome could have been any different. I decided the answer was no. The Universe had a plan that was beyond my understanding at the time. What did Pee Wee die from? The cruel irony was she had gone out in that paddock on her own and most likely had been bitten by a snake. I relaxed and accepted everything that had evolved over those few days. I learnt a lesson in the value of getting out of my head from the negative emotions I was swamping myself with for the positive outcome of finding my mate.

How did I achieve this?

I simply moved my focus from my head to my heart. Pee Wee passed less than six months ago as I write. Since that time, I frequently consciously move focus from my head to my heart, especially at any time I recognize myself experiencing negative thoughts or emotions. The results are truly very satisfying to experience, both in life outcomes and in the feeling of peacefulness in my body. New positive people have come into my life, support for my projects has turned up from out of the blue and, in particular, my intuition has become stronger as I notice, recognize and acknowledge signs from the Universe all around me. Signs appear through dreams, people, birds, animals, books, music ... the list goes on. In general, there is a peacefulness I feel within that was never in existence before. I am blessed.

The method to move focus from head to heart area to me is very simple. Perhaps you may like to use and adapt this method to how it feels most comfortable to you. This is an exercise that takes just seconds, and no one is the wiser. No need to even close your eyes or to even be in a quiet place!

1. First of all acknowledge to yourself your attention (thoughts, emotions) is coming from your head.
2. Next acknowledge to yourself how much better you feel overall when living from your heart area.

3. Now, with Intention, pretend to "look" into your head and feel/see/hear/sense or otherwise the tightness of the judgment/resentment/anger/or whatever emotion or thoughts are causing you to be operating at a low frequency energy.

4. Now, again using Intention, pretend to "look" down into your heart area to place your focus there. Perhaps have a target spot and see/feel/hear/sense or otherwise the relief in your heart area.

5. Hold this focus for as long as you can, and use whatever sense feels best for you to notice the better feeling of changing from lower to higher frequency energy from moving into your heart area.

6. The trick is, as with almost any exercise, to do this with consistency. Even flip into your head and back to your heart area for no reason! As you do this "flipping" up and down, down and up, frequently, you will find you begin to clearly notice the times you are in your head and attached to lower frequency energies. When you do notice, with having done this exercise frequently, you will pop into your heart area with ease and grace, and stay there for longer and longer intervals.

Many animals have appeared throughout my life to teach me valuable lessons. Pee Wee was one of those teachers. In earlier years, I basically never recognized these lessons for what they were. These days deep understanding has surfaced of why some of those lessons were repeated again and again.

In the same way men and women carry both the testosterone and estrogen hormones, so do we also carry both the Divine Masculine and Divine Feminine energies. In the same way we frequently have hormone imbalances, so also are our divine energies also frequently imbalanced. I was a classic example.

The circumstances of Pee Wee's passing activated a major change in my life. My outlook on life and others has softened. Previously I would be quite aggressive, very competitive, wanting to be the best, and I was very good at passing judgment on others and dosing out tough love. In other words, I was living predominantly in masculine energies.

As our current times draw upon us to reunite with our Divine Feminine energy, Pee Wee activated that choice for change in me, although I did not realize it at the time. All I knew was my heart needed to soften to allow assistance from Divine Guidance to find dear Pee Wee. As I came to a place where I was out of options to find Pee Wee, I bowed down in resignation and called on the Universe for help. As low frequency energies were recognized and released, I moved into my heart and therefore into my Divine Feminine energies. I was now living in Love and open to Divine Guidance.

Over the previous year or so, I had been accessing and receiving Divine Guidance off and on, yet I did not recognize it for what it truly was. These days, as I continue to consciously recognize and increasingly live in my Divine Feminine energies, my life is flowing with an ease and grace never before experienced. Holding this state is allowing me to further develop my skills in connecting to nature and receiving messages from many sources as I evolve as The Cosmic Connector.

May you find your own healing in reading Pee Wee's story. I feel so blessed to be here on Earth at this time as we all evolve towards living in a balanced world of the Divine Masculine and Divine Feminine energies.

LINDA MURRAY lives in Australia after migrating from New Zealand. Whether city or country, nature is large in her life. Linda develops your understanding of nature's messages given through weeds, bugs, disease, and animals. Choose earth-friendly ways and energies for step-by-step soil nutrition and health. Healthy soil is our legacy, our lifeblood and conduit to health. Linda shares how "dancing with nature" is a balancing act. HTTP://WWW.CARBICULTURE.COM is her knowledge hub and has lots of free advice.

 LINDA'S FREE GIFT: Sally My Teacher eBook, a beautiful animal story at HTTP://EMBRACEDBYTHEDIVINE.COM/GET-YOUR-BONUS-GIFTS/

Open Your Mind and Say Ahhhhhhhh!
– Steps to Capsize a Crisis
– Janet Parsons

Life at 45 was feeling pretty fantastic! I had started a publishing company and my first children's picture book, *The Five Senses of Love,* had won two literary awards in the USA, made the Premier's reading list in three states in Australia and the rights had been sold and translated into Korean.

Rights for a bi-lingual Mandarin edition were underway and a large New York publishing house had ordered a 10,000-copy print run to be in stores in the USA by December 2012.

My foray into publishing had occurred with no platform, no distributor and pretty much no idea.

However, I had read Louise Hay's journey into publishing and was encouraged to give it a red-hot go.

The manuscript for *The Five Senses of Love* had been really well received in educational and family psychology sectors. I enlisted professional editing services, sourced an exceptional young illustrator, jumped on a plane to Hong Kong, found myself a reliable, ethical printing firm and Potoroo Publishing was up and away.

The books arrived and I sent them to all the major Australian papers, received five-star reviews and stumbled into Dennis Jones and Associates, distribution agents.

I remember that Dennis queried the choice of block color cover at the time and I told him I needed the block color so that the award stickers had a great backdrop. He laughed and agreed they would love to take on my book.

Dennis suggested I pitch the book to Rod and Mary Hare at the Australian Licencing Corporation.

I now had international representation.

Sounds like happily ever after, doesn't it?

A Funny Thing Happened on the Way Out of the Shower...

As I emerged from the shower on Thursday September 21, 2012, I discovered a lump in my right breast.

One week later it was confirmed that I had breast cancer. I was faced with two choices for coping with the road ahead: fear or love.

I chose love, and the journey that ensued and continues for me is, in a word, spectacular!

The previous 17 years of reading, meditating and having an addiction to all things self-help served as a life apprenticeship.

Well, the time had truly arrived to help myself.

The "Art" of Being Blindsided 101

The initial blindside impact is experienced uniquely by each soul.

Each time you receive the type of news that blindsides you, including and not limited to: death, divorce, disease and dire straits in general – your reaction will be different.

At times, I have literally been floored by certain news; I have had to physically lie down to assimilate what I am hearing. This has happened in several locations that are not ideal settings for lying down. This has caused some consternation to the news bearers, however I listen to my body, and what other people think is really none of my business anyway.

It is at these moments in life that you will need to exercise *intensive care of self and soul.*

The more intensive care you can extend to this phase of circumstance, the better.

Severe shock and grief can cause many physical, emotional and spiritual disruptions. It is not a time to "soldier on" or "push through." Open your heart and receive the love, care and support that friends, family and professionals are offering.

If you have no one in these circles please call the support services in your area.

Human kindness is a deep well and there will always be a helping hand for those who ask.

Allow your physical body to process the pain and all the symptoms that come with it.

Ensure that you are supplementing your diet during this intensive care period. If you are uninterested in or unable to keep up with a nourishing food intake, source a protein powder that has added vitamins and minerals. Effective and easily digestible, this is a lifesaver when it comes to staying nourished. This will help your immune system, which can become vulnerable when stressed.

As the old adage goes, "Put on your own oxygen mask first, before you assist anyone else."

Consult with your health professionals as soon as you are able to make an appointment. Have someone accompany you, as the other person can take notes and even take over if you become too overwhelmed to speak.

Crying in a warm shower or bath is a wonderful physical release. Warm water relaxes muscles and soothes body aches. Adding a cup of Epsom Salts is a great addition to a soak in the tub, as are essential oils such as lavender, rose and geranium. Make sure you read the directions on the oil bottles for correct dosage.

Homeopathic remedies for shock, grief and trauma, such as Bach's Rescue Remedy, available as drops, spray or pastilles, are excellent and are essential to have in your home's first aid kit.

The benefits of exercise are inestimable. As a coping mechanism for stress and anxiety, it is part of nature's own survival kit. Just a few of the benefits are:

Reduce stress

Ward off anxiety and feelings of depression

Boost self-esteem

Improve sleep

"The best way out is through."
~ Robert Frost

Once you have regained the strength to stand, it is time to work through whatever has blindsided you.

I will share some stepping stones to help you make your way along the path of love and not fear.

"I learned that courage was not the absence of fear, but the
triumph over it. The brave man is not he who does not feel afraid,
but he who conquers that fear."
~ Nelson Mandela

When deciding which course of treatment to undergo for my breast cancer I had several conversations and did a lot of research around many Eastern and Western medicinal regimes. Several of the Eastern-based philosophies involved lengthy time away and most were abroad. I had conversations with several women who had experienced great success with these options, however the fears that led to their choices were still present even five years on.

It was at that time that I decided on a combined effort. I had the lump removed and when pathology results indicated a lymph node was involved, I had a wide axillary clearance. Axillary clearance involves removing several or all of the lymph nodes from the armpit.

A full body scan followed. This was clear – YIPPEE!

Six rounds of chemotherapy and five weeks of radiotherapy were now recommended as *adjuvant therapy*. Adjuvant therapy for breast cancer is designed to treat micro-metastatic disease, or breast cancer cells that have escaped the breast.

I decided to proceed with this treatment and at the same time enlist my holistic team to ensure I supported my system as best I could. My naturopath, who specializes in women's health, assured me that I could go through this treatment without nausea, fatigue, pain, weight-loss, taste loss and the rest of the lengthy list of side effects. True to her words, I sailed through without any of these physical symptoms.

NB: I showed my oncologist the supplement list and dosage prior to starting treatment.

I sought a general practitioner who specializes in the support of cancer patients and who provides a vitamin B injection the day before each chemotherapy infusion. I found this to be really beneficial for my energy levels. It was wonderful to have my naturopath checking on my blood levels during treatment and seeing that my immune system was in high performance mode for the duration.

The one side effect I did experience was hair loss. I will go into that later – as it turns out, this was quite an ally for the personal growth work I was about to undertake. There is something so raw, vulnerable and yet so very beautiful, looking at your bald reflection.

Open Your Mind and Say Ahhhhhhhh

"Meditation makes the entire nervous system go into a field of coherence."
~ *Deepak Chopra*

On the day that I had the biopsy results to confirm the cancer and the resulting planned treatment, I remember sitting down to our family dinner table and my middle daughter asking,

"How are you going to get through this?"

"You know how I've been meditating? Well I'm going to AHHHH my way through." was my answer.

The AHHHH comes from a repeated mantra in some guided meditations.

I had noticed that the regular practice of meditation had improved every area of my life. The way I experienced stressful work conversations and events was helped when I meditated. My reaction to the general life issues that can cause blood to boil was diffused with meditation.

During treatment, I meditated up to three times a day. I always use a guided meditation. There is a plethora of these to choose from. I suggest you have a few on hand to mix it up. They are available to purchase on iTunes or at your local bookstore or library.

The peace you experience for mind, body and soul is incredibly nourishing.

My 18-year-old daughter, who had asked the question about how I was going to get through the situation, had recently taken up meditation. When I asked her what she was enjoying most, she explained that after a meditation she feels *reborn*.

Powerful and effective, you too will achieve brilliant results with practice.

Fifteen minutes a day to fortify your whole being.

Bring It On.

Calling All Angels

> "If you knew who walked beside you on this path that you
> have chosen, fear would be impossible."
> ~ A Course in Miracles

Your angels love to help you through this life every step of the way.

Call on them, even if you don't believe in them or if you struggle to believe in them. Call on them even if you subscribe to no belief system.

They believe in you.

HERE IS A BRIEF DIRECTORY FOR YOU TO KNOW WHOM TO CALL UPON:

ARCHANGEL MICHAEL – Clears away lower energies of fear. Ask him to stay with you if anxious.

ARCHANGEL RAPHAEL – Healing powers for all living things.

ARCHANGEL CHAMUEL – For peace, personally and globally.

ARCHANGEL URIEL – For ideas and intellectual guidance. Great when you are studying.

ARCHANGEL AZRAEL – Helps with grieving and assistance for those called to counsel.

ARCHANGEL ZADKIEL – Clears away emotional blocks in your heart.

ARCHANGEL JOPHIEL – For clearing physical space, redecorating or spring-cleaning.

ARCHANGEL ARIEL – To boost your confidence and courage.

ARCHANGEL GABRIEL – Helps writers and journalists deliver healing messages.

ARCHANGEL RAGUEL – Guides actions to be fair and just.

ARCHANGEL SANDALPHON – Associated with music. Encourages gentle action and words.

ARCHANGEL JEREMIEL – Helps make life reviews, release of old habits.

ARCHANGEL HANIEL – Helps with our natural cycles, moods and rhythms. Encourages self-appreciation.

ARCHANGEL RAZIEL – Call on Raziel to help turn your ideas into gold.

ARCHANGEL METATRON – For help with children. Clears psychic toxins from your body and chakras.

Look for messages that come in sequences of three. These signs can come in from all your senses. Be awake and aware. Feathers in unusual places are often a sign that angels are nearby. As are repeated numbers. I encourage you to learn as much as you can about these amazing friends of ours.

You are never, ever alone.

"Taffirmations:" Tapping into the Good Stuff

Tapping as a healing methodology is buzzing right now, and deservedly so.

About seven years ago, I had developed a chronic phobia about driving through tunnels. I had a panic attack in a tunnel about six years earlier and had not been able to drive in a tunnel and was getting anxiety even driving on freeways. I had one session of EFT (Emotional Freedom Technique or tapping) with a qualified psychologist and drove home from the session through a major road tunnel and pulled into the emergency lane – not in panic – in excitement, to call my husband and tell him what I had done. I implore you, open your mind to this modality and read on as to how I came up with my version of EFT, which I call "Taffirmations."

Louise Hay's little blue book, *Heal Your Body,* has a list of physical ailments and beside them provides the appropriate affirmation to engage healing in the afflicted areas.

I combined the EFT points with Louise's affirmations and used a mirror. The affirmations I used were for breast problems and cancer. I would look into the mirror and say the affirmation while tapping the EFT point. There are many resources for learning about tapping. Look it up on the internet and you will be given many choices. To begin with, I would recommend finding a qualified therapist to teach you the processes and then you can adapt them to suit yourself.

As I mentioned earlier, doing this with a completely bald head i.e. no hair, eyelashes or brows, was at first confronting. Over time, though, I found it gave me strength and a profound appreciation for who I am and what I was working through.

Find Your Grail

"Hawaii is not a state of mind, but a state of grace."
~ Paul Theroux

The islands of Hawaii have been referred to as "the spiritual navel of Mother Earth." I have been traveling regularly to this destination for over 25 years. Every time I arrive I feel like I have been called home. The beauty of these islands and their people is phenomenal.

Of the many healing practices I have learned during this time, there are two that I will now share. Many brilliant holistic techniques are practiced by these folk. They are easy to implement wherever you may be located, to bring the Aloha spirit into your life.

Ha – The Breath of Life

Ha breathing is a simple, yet incredibly effective, way to replenish and reconnect to universal energy. To begin, inhale through your nose to a count of three or four. Next, exhale through your mouth to a count of six or eight making a soft *haaaaaa* sound. The inhale/exhale is always at a one to two ratio (i.e. three counts of inhale = six counts of exhale).

Standing with your feet shoulder-width apart outside on some earth or grass provides a great grounding connection. You may find it more comfortable to sit or lay down. If you cannot get outside, just close your eyes and imagine a lush, beautiful piece of grassy earth. Hold out your arms to each side with palms facing upward.

How long should you do this? In a perfect world and if the elders were in charge, you would do continuous ha breathing for days at a time to build up energy for any big project.

For those of us running on everyday human time, I recommend doing this breathing for several minutes each day and longer if you are facing a situation that will require more energy from you.

Forgive to Live – Forgiveness is the Key to Unlocking the Life You Desire and Deserve

*"To forgive is to set a prisoner free and discover
that the prisoner was you."*
~ Lewis B. Smedes

The second piece of support gleaned from my time in Hawaii is the practice of *Ho'oponopono* (pronounced Ho-o-pono-pono), a forgiveness ritual that incorporates four magic sentences:

I am sorry.
Please forgive me.
I love you.
I thank you.

If anything in life is troubling you, please give your thoughts and efforts to the above mantra. It could be a person, a situation, a place or even a memory. This mantra operates through time and space, even beyond cause and effect.

Print them out and keep them on you. I have a business card-sized laminated copy that I carry in my wallet.

There are many excellent books that further explore the Ho'oponopono method. A little blue book titled *Ho'oponopono* by Ulrich E. Dupree is a simple and effective manual.

Those who are familiar with Louise Hay's work will be aware of the vital ingredient that forgiveness and releasing of our past, plays in living this life to the full. The Hawaiian exercise above, to me, encapsulates Louise's findings.

Old Dog, New Tricks? – You Bet

"As long as you live, keep learning how to live."
~ Lucius Annaeus Seneca

As I come to the close of this chapter I implore that if you are in the midst of a crisis or find yourself as the carer for someone in a crisis, you take from this book any tools that please you.

There are many highly effective modalities to assist you in capsizing a crisis. Remember the intensive care mode and be especially kind to yourself through this stage. And truth be told, I recommend practicing *kindness to self* for the rest of your days.

Many of these tools *are outside the square*. I call for you to open your mind and leave fear and judgments behind.

I will leave you with a story that happened to me after my first chemo treatment. I had enjoyed some reflexology in Hawaii a couple of weeks before starting chemo, and thought another reflexology session would be a nice treat. I found a local clinic and when I arrived, my practitioner came to greet me. Kesang was a tiny Tibetan lady, gently spoken and graceful of movement. As we entered her beautifully lit and exotically fragrant treatment room, I sat in the comfortable chair. She asked what I felt I needed today, as she practiced several therapies.

I explained that I was heading in tomorrow for my second round of chemotherapy and I felt that another reflexology session might be relaxing.

She smiled a warm smile and said in a soft voice that perhaps I would like a Tibetan peace massage.

That sounded like heaven to my ears. She placed her hands on my shoulders and asked that I close my eyes. She moved from my shoulders to my head and to parts of my back and legs and feet. It was a gentle channeled healing.

When finished, she took my hand and said, "Tomorrow, when you arrive at the hospital, leave your fear at the door. Trade it in for wondrous gratitude. Give thanks with a heart wide open for all the doctors, nurses, scientists, drug manufacturers and the millions of souls whose lives have gone before you. Look at the bags of medicine with love. Love pouring through the tubes into your body. All love and all gratitude. In the end Janet, it will not be Western or Eastern medicine that saves your life. Your healing must come from within."

As the tears flowed from my closed eyes I felt those words resonate in every cell of my being.

JANET PARSONS is an award-winning writer of stories and songs, with most ideas coming in at 3 a.m. when other people are sleeping soundly. The youngest of 13 children, she believes her imagination was fed by a healthy diet observing the antics of her siblings and being fuelled with great literature in a TV-free home. She lives in magnificent Melbourne, Australia, with her husband, children and enough wildlife to start a zoo. Janet is currently working on her third children's book, a non-fiction novel and the first in a fiction series and is consequently fairly sleep deprived. Follow Janet through her blog http://potorooprose.wordpress.com

 **WIN A FREE COPY** of *The Five Senses of Love.* Details at HTTP://EMBRACEDBYTHEDIVINE.COM/GET-YOUR-BONUS-GIFTS/

Listening to the Voice Within
– Andrea Beadle

Throughout my working life I always felt that there was "something missing." I always loved a new challenge but the excitement of a new job would always wear off pretty quickly and I would find myself "bored" once I felt I had learned what I could from a role.

I had a successful career and was promoted very quickly and many times; however, within a year to 18 months of a promotion or new job, I always found myself looking for something new to keep my attention.

I thrived in high-pressure environments as long as there was a shiny, new thing to play with. Promotion, starting a new project, dealing with a major crisis such as a store burning down … but once the excitement wore off, there I was again.

No matter what I did, I always found myself feeling that that there was that something missing again.

In my late 20s I gave up my career and traveled extensively which gave me a wonderful feeling of freedom and I learnt so much about myself in the process. With the help of my travel companion (now my husband), I dealt with many of my demons and returned home with more confidence.

University, teaching and more travel followed until I found myself in a job that I felt happy with for longer than I had ever done in the past.

Mid-Life Crisis?

However, as a successful career woman in my late 30s, my world was turned upside down after the birth of my son in 2005 – and from that point on I found things gradually building to what eventually became breaking point.

I had always been successful at everything I turned my hand to and I imagined that with my skills I would find being a mother a breeze.

How wrong can one girl be? While I loved my new son unconditionally and adored being with him, financially I had to return to work when he was seven months old. As an older mum, I knew I could not work full-time and leave him in childcare all week. There was no point in having waited so long for him if I did that!

So I determined to work part-time and have the best of both worlds. How hard could that be?

I could never have imagined how much of a struggle it would be to balance all the different areas of my life! How could a successful career girl find it so difficult? I found myself being pulled in all different directions … feeling guilty when I was at work and not being able to concentrate on my son fully when I wasn't.

The house was a mess, I battled the baby blues and all the time I was wishing I could be at home, like many of my friends in more fortunate financial circumstances.

I knew that I needed to leave my job. My heart told me, my gut told me and yet I couldn't! I didn't know how. I didn't believe I could!

I felt trapped for so many reasons. Money was a big one. I didn't know how we would survive if I gave up my job so I thought about a new job. But that just filled me with dread.

At least I was where I was safe. I knew who I was and it was comfortable. Where else would I find the flexibility I had with a good salary and recognition? I just couldn't see it.

But I knew something had to change. I knew I was dying inside and I ignored it. Not because I didn't want things to change but because I didn't know how. My days at work were painfully dull. I was tired, irritable and sometimes it felt as if my whole world was being dragged slowly into a black hole and I was powerless to escape its pull. Deep down I knew that something had to drastically change.

And it did!

Slowly my health began to trouble me. I didn't know what was happening but each month I began to experience increasingly more painful periods. They began to get so bad that I couldn't get out of bed in the morning without taking strong painkillers first.

The pain often made me sick, sometimes I would pass out, and, for a few days each month, the crippling pain meant I couldn't function without strong painkillers. I began to have to take time off work and although I knew something wasn't right, I soldiered on regardless.

Until one day I read an article about endometriosis. The words hit me like a bolt of lightning and I knew this was what I was suffering from.

In February 2010 there followed a rapid surgical diagnosis that left me totally reeling. The second child that we had hoped for was never going to happen and I was told that I would need a total hysterectomy.

Shocked, I retreated into a period where I wallowed in self-pity.

There was something about being told I needed a hysterectomy that shook me to the core. It felt as if my identity as a woman was threatened and that was something I was going to fight!

The self-pity was shoved to one side and a fierce warrior woman emerged from deep within, determined to fight this condition and the prognosis I had been given.

I began to research the condition and seemed to intuitively know that I needed to turn to nutrition to help. I began to work with an amazing nutritionist who helped me to dramatically reduce the pain that I was experiencing to the point that, within a couple of months, I was able to go to work on just paracetamol. It felt like a miracle to me.

The improvement in my health meant that I fought with the surgeon to avoid a total hysterectomy and he agreed to try a less drastic approach. However, come the day of my surgery in August 2010, the news wasn't good.

When they operated, my insides were a mess and they had to abort the surgery.

I was told that everything was stuck together. My bladder was upside down, back to front and stuck to my uterus. My bowel was badly affected and they were very concerned that if I didn't agree to the more radical surgery that I could lose one of my kidneys, which was also being affected.

So once again, I prepared for the surgery that I had fought against.

In the meantime, I had been away from work for two separate periods of time and had prepared to hand over my responsibilities for a prolonged period of time away from work.

My surgery was rescheduled for October, and although I continued working until that time, I found that I was relinquishing the hold that my work had had over me.

I began working with an energy healer and did work with a number of coaches as well as exploring every holistic therapy and energy healing modality I could find.

A friend also told me that if I didn't deal with the underlying energetic and emotional issues, my condition would just return. I recognized that the biggest part of my healing was going to be on an emotional level. I knew that I needed to do a lot of inner work in order to prepare emotionally for my surgery and the months that were to follow.

I delved deep and explored a lot of issues during the next few months. The awakening process that had started with the birth of my son was turned up to full speed and I reconnected with some of the things that I had loved as a young woman. My intuition became stronger and refused to be ignored any longer and it was as if I was taking a crash course in spiritual matters, particularly the laws of the Universe and manifestation. It was as if every lesson I learned was played out in my life at full speed. If I thought about something it happened. Each lesson I was learning played out with people around me so that I really "got it." It was both terrifying and magical to see the power of beliefs and thought in action.

It was an emotional roller coaster, but I handed my surgery over to the Divine and trusted that all would be in my highest good. I remember going down to surgery repeating an affirmation in my head over and over and over again. Somehow it helped me to remain calm and gave me a sense of peace. I guess, looking back, it helped me to just accept what was going on without worrying about the outcome. I visualized the surgeons only acting in my highest good and just trusted.

I also visualized that all of the issues and negative beliefs I had were all rolled up into a ball and placed within my uterus so that when the surgeons operated the issues and negative beliefs were also removed.

I determined that this was the beginning of a new chapter of my life.

The surgery went well and in the early hours of the following morning I was awoken by the sound of a beautiful voice calling my name. There was no one in the room. There was no one outside of the room. I've never heard the voice since, but it was so clear and so real. Not like being awoken from a dream where the voice is inside the dream, but it was physically present with me. I believe that I handed my surgery over to the Divine and in that moment I was being shown that I was being watched over.

Accept Support

Before I was discharged my surgeon gave me a very stern warning. Because my surgery had been keyhole it was easy to forget how serious the operation was.

I was to do nothing for a week. No lifting, no carrying. I had to take it easy. Nothing unusual about that … it is the same after any surgery. However, he gave me a warning that I couldn't ignore. There was a very real danger that if I overdid it I could experience septic shock because of the nature of my surgery. He gave me a list of symptoms that I should look out for and said that, if I noticed those symptoms, I should present immediately to hospital … adding that it could be fatal within hours if I did not.

As a woman who had been fiercely independent, this was probably the only thing that would have stopped me trying to carry on regardless of my surgery. For once in my life I really did have to stop and let in the help and support that was always there for me, but that I was too stubborn to ask for.

My recovery went as expected and I continued to work on myself, albeit facing my demons through many tears. There were highs and lows in dealing with the emotional roller coaster of losing my femininity. Terrified that the surgery would ruin my relationship with my husband and wondering if I would ever be able to have or enjoy sex again.

And all the time in the background there was the looming prospect of having to return to work. My anticipated recovery meant that I should be back at work in three months. This was like a time bomb that was constantly ticking in my ear.

More soul searching ensued. This time I started looking at my life and evaluating where I was. I knew that I was unhappy, but I didn't know what I wanted any more. When you are in the middle of a dark night of the soul, it is hard to know which way to turn.

The only thing that I knew was that I wanted to be able to walk my son to school every day. I wanted to be there for him when he came home from school and I knew I wanted a life built around him rather than the false career that I had built for myself. My career had defined me and I didn't want that any more. I wasn't the same person that I had been before my son was born. Something huge had shifted and I needed to find the real me under all the labels that I had given myself.

Every day that I walked my son to school during my recovery I gave thanks for having this time to be able to take him to school. I focused on being present in the moment, including listening to the birds singing, enjoying the sunshine on my face. When it rained, I imagined the rain washing away any negative emotions. And gradually I began to build a vision for what I wanted my life to look like.

I knew my vision didn't include going back to work but I still didn't know how I could make that happen. Instead of telling myself that I couldn't leave my job or trying to work out how, I began to wonder how it might be possible. This simple way of looking at things enables you to start to remove blinkers that prevent you from seeing solutions.

I clearly remember one day in January 2011. I was at home and became very upset about financially not being able to give up work. I had broken down and cried before making three decisions:

To give up my job…

For life to be easy…

To be financially secure…

Looking at the three decisions I couldn't see how they were all possible. Giving up my job seemed to be impossible when you looked at the other two! Instead of saying that it wasn't possible I handed it over to the Divine and asked for everything to be taken care of.

That night my husband came home and could see that I had been crying. It led to a long conversation about our financial situation that totally shattered the financial illusion that we had been living in.

Instantly we went from thinking we were financially trapped with me needing to work, to seeing that it was totally an illusion. We had choices and it was liberating!

Fast-forward a short while to the time that I was supposed to be going back to work. Physically my health was good, but emotionally I was still struggling with the thought of going back to my job. Emotionally, I had decided that I needed to leave, financially there were now options, but I was still struggling to know what to do.

I had tried to visit my office at Christmas, but had broken down in tears on the way and couldn't bring myself to go in. So I had a very emotional, but frank conversation with my boss, letting her know that I was really struggling. I even told her through my tears that if there were a redundancy package on the table that I would have taken it. However, there were no redundancies at that time. We agreed that I would rehabilitate by going back to work in a different part of the organization while we evaluated options.

On the first day that I went into the new office it was as if my body had different ideas. It knew that I had made the decision that I needed to leave. I walked in and within half an hour I was literally shaking and feeling so ill that I had to be sent home. I was shaking so hard that my hands could hardly grip the steering wheel.

The next few months saw what I could only consider to be a miraculous manifestation of me expressing my thoughts to my boss. Amazingly, I managed to secure a redundancy package through a shake-up, which didn't affect our department, as long as a space was held open for someone who was at risk of redundancy elsewhere in the organization.

This gave me part of the solution that enabled me to leave and to be financially supported whilst I started my own business as a coach.

It was not all plain sailing, but there were many other instances of me thinking of something and the solution appearing, as if by magic. I learned not to try to control the outcome. I learned to be open to solutions appearing out of nowhere and I learned that if you suspend belief and look for a way out, one will appear.

I also learned to look out for the messages that the Divine is trying to send us. If we are closed to the messages and try and work it all out ourselves, it is so much harder.

I began working as a coach, but didn't really get any clients. However, people started to ask me to build websites for them. Initially my thoughts were that I didn't want to do this. I'd tried building websites as a way to leave my job a few years before, but it had never really worked. The competition would always undercut me and I had no point of difference.

Suddenly, I had people offering to pay me to do this without me even trying to get work. I was reminded by a good friend that I needed to take notice of what I was being shown. It might not have worked before but this time something was different.

Slowly but surely a new body of work began to appear for me. Through the work I was doing on websites for holistic practitioners and spiritual business owners, I discovered my true work. The websites were the thing that people knew they needed, but in reality they needed so much more.

This work enabled me to combine all of the skills that I had developed over my career and to embrace my spirituality and intuitive coaching. It is forever shifting as I change and grow, but the core is about helping people to find their purpose and to express it through their business to help heal the world.

My health is greatly improved and continues to improve as I embrace the real me, listen to my intuition and connect with Source in my work.

My fears about my hysterectomy affecting my relationship with my husband did initially cause some problems, but working through the beliefs that were in the way and going through a great deal of turbulence enabled us to rebuild our relationship on stronger foundations. It has not been an easy ride, but I continued to apply the lessons that I learned and our relationship grows stronger each day.

Lessons

I hope that the lessons that I have learned on my journey might help to inspire change in your own lives.

1) LISTEN TO YOUR HEART, TO YOUR GUT, TO YOUR BODY

If you ignore them for long enough you will get hit by the proverbial truck! For me, ignoring what my heart and my gut knew for so long ended up in my body having to literally stop me in my tracks to prevent me from going back to work. You know what is true for you. Stress, anxiety, pain, depression and physical ailments are messages for you to stop and take a look at what is wrong in your life. Listen to them. Tune in. Ask what you truly want from life.

2) WE ALWAYS HAVE CHOICES

During my surgery, although I didn't realize the significance at the time, I made a choice that this was to be a turning point for me. That it was the beginning of a new chapter in my life. We can look at the same situation from a number of different perspectives and each perspective will influence the way we go forwards. Always ask yourself if you are choosing the most positive perspective that you can. It does make a difference.

3) ACCEPT SUPPORT

So many women try to do it all alone. They soldier on, don't ask for help and end up resenting other people for not helping them. We readily help others and give freely of our own time but are uncomfortable allowing ourselves to receive the same kind of support that we give out. Allow people to help. They want to and enjoy doing so. Notice when you turn help away and recognize that you are turning away the gift of someone's time when you say no.

4) KNOW WHAT YOU WANT

Knowing what you want is the key to changing your life. Without knowing where you are going you will keep walking around in circles. Create a vision for yourself and recognize each moment of each day where you already have something that is part of your vision. So often we focus on what we want in the future without recognising the parts of our life that we want to keep.

5) MAKE THE DECISION!

The power of making a decision should never be underestimated. If we know what we want we often think that we have decided to get it. However, energetically we can often be out of alignment. Actually make a firm decision that you want something. The stronger the decision, the quicker things will begin to happen around you to make it so. Also be aware that when you decide, things can often seem to be showing you that it isn't possible. I see these as the roadblocks that you need to navigate showing you your beliefs and the issues that you need to work on to have what you want. Don't give up!

6) FOLLOW THE SIGNS

Once you've made a decision about what you want, don't think you need to do it all alone. When we try to figure things out we can often stop the flow. Ask the Divine to help you. Think about me with the websites. I was focused on coaching, but was shown that websites were the way forward for me. If I had ignored what was going on I would have made things hard for myself. Messages will appear, but if you are ignoring them, you can miss important opportunities.

ANDREA BEADLE (United Kingdom) helps heart-centred entrepreneurs find their purpose and create the business that is the expression of their soul. She believes that your business will only grow as far as you grow as an individual and, using Higher Guidance Coaching, helps you to break through the beliefs that are holding you back so that you can have a healthy life and a healthy business. She is creating the Heart Business Academy for heart-centered entrepreneurs at WWW.ANDREABEADLE.COM

 ANDREA'S FREE GIFT: Audit Your Life eBook and mp3 at HTTP://EMBRACEDBYTHEDIVINE.COM/GET-YOUR-BONUS-GIFTS/

Lovingly Letting You Go

– Brenda Pearce

Ours was a marriage ignited with hopes and dreams, of children unborn, and life yet unlived. There was hope. There was promise. There was love.

Three years into our marriage our hopes of children were dashed by miscarriage, and jagged months of false-positive pregnancy results. Of testing by doctors, still left with no understanding as to why children were not conceived. Little did I realize the stress that we were immersed in: "Me" with a full-time shift working job; "He" with the day-to-day unyielding demands of operating a dairy farm. There was little rest, little recreation, and a whole lot of stress, and wanting and desiring children put us both into even greater stress. It was a frenzy of building, creating, and growing personally, yet stymied for lack of our ultimate goal and gift of love – a child!

Finally, after months of anticipation and no results, our fertility doctor suggested a medication to help with the process. At last, my babies may be possible. I took the prescription home and followed directions, and our hopes and dreams became a glimmer of possibility – then anticipation – for the dreamed-of children of our hearts, minds and desires.

With the fragile thread of two weeks past the due period, I began to glow with the Mona Lisa smile of someone with a great secret yet unshared. I noted a new fullness beginning and I wanted to be sure before I even shared this with my husband. Our baby was now a possibility; an anticipated hope and dream filled with wishes and prayers.

It was in these fragile few beginning weeks that the heart and lungs were in their early stages of development. When the embryo became a zygote and the cells were multiplying rapidly in the flow of the miracle of life, not one but two beautiful beings of love were being created ... little to my knowledge.

It was during these early weeks that my beloved husband suffered a devastating farming accident. He was knocked off of his milking stool by an angry, highly strung cow and he fell into the metal railing dividing that cow and the next cow. He ended up with a broken neck. This injury is known as a hangman's neck fracture at the C1 and C2 levels of his cervical spine.

Our hopes and dreams of our lives unfolding with years of abundance spiraled down into weeks of chaos and uncertainty from the shock of the accident. Despite the miracles of modern emergency protocol, there were weeks of hospitalization, traction, surgical intervention and pain, pain, pain. A vital, young, strong, and fearless man had to adjust to the robotic, unmoving world of burr holes, metal frames, limited mobility, and an uncertain future.

It was immediately after the accident and during the first few days of stabilization that I went to our family doctor to inform him of what had occurred to my husband, and to get a pregnancy test to confirm the pregnancy. Out of concern for the incredible shock of the events of the accident, I was immediately scheduled for the first of several ultrasounds, which confirmed the presence of twins! Mixed with the torn emotions of my, now-announced and burgeoning pregnancy was both great sorrow and great joy. Great shock!

Fraternal and present in their worlds of embryonic fluid, they were implanted in two distinct, different parts of the private uterine world, nurtured, pure and pristine. One was slightly larger than the other, but that was not a concern as conception of two separate ova had occurred in their own divine timing. Our babies – the fruits of love, hope and joy – were now maturing in the midst of pain, sorrow and uncertainty.

This occurrence was the panacea that my husband needed to endure all that he needed to go through. The hope and joy of life to come provided him with encouragement to endure months of immobility.

We were certainly an odd couple: me very pregnant, and he with his halo brace on, going to obstetrician visits and neurologist visits together.

A whirl of medical appointments and procedures, ultrasounds, and halo pin adjustments ensued. With three months to go until the twins were to be born, we were devastated to discover that his neck had not healed and that surgery was required to fuse it. We endured this news together with Faith, hope and prayer, cemented with love.

One grueling, storm-filled, February day, surgery was done successfully! The months of the halo brace and pins into the skull were over, although the full effect and limitations thereof were still unknown. The awkward positioning of frozen immobility was finally over. Never once did he complain. Never once did he give up hope. The man I loved was my hero. My inspiration!

Although there were still the hurdles of healing for him, it was now my time to relax and enjoy the remaining months of my preparation for the joyously anticipated births. Ultrasounds confirmed that my two beautiful babies were on track – they were healthy, growing and doing everything expected in the great succession of development. We were healing, and the anticipation was exciting. The beautiful stirrings of life in development! Stretching, moving, growing and loved. Our reward after months of uncertainty!

However, it was during one night that both my husband and I received a gift from the Divine, a dream so real and so vivid and so strong. A forewarning of what we would go through, we were blessed to receive this warning. Both a preparation and a blessing, we awakened simultaneously and simply looked at each other in shock. The look in his eyes mirroring my own, we both unveiled the dream that we had had. One of our babies was not well, and would not be with us for long. We both, simultaneously, knew which one it was and placed our hands on the child in the upper right quadrant, bowed our heads and cried. Our shock and dismay and pain as to why the Divine would so gift us, and then warn us of what would occur?

What was this cruel joke that would have us both dreaming of this warning, of this impending crisis that was still to come and of the pain that would enter our lives? What had we so done to deserve this? We bowed our heads in prayer.

Further doctor appointments and another ultrasound did not reveal any medical concerns. The doctors tried to allay our concerns, but an inner knowing could not dispel the medical findings. Yet, our family doctor did say that despite the babies' positive growth in utero, multiple births were high risk and, more times than not, something could occur that was not anticipated.

Heavy hearted, now warned and prepared both medically and divinely, we were both aware of risks and challenges that lay ahead. With one month to go, I went into early labor. Bed rest and hospitalization were the keys to buy further precious days in utero for the babies to strengthen, grow and mature.

However, on May 21, 1988, Twin A and Twin B were born. There was no stopping Twin A. A breach, but very healthy, Kevin Philip was born screaming and healthy at 5lbs 11oz. The NICU (Neonatal Intensive Care Unit) team that was present included a former colleague of mine, Margaret. The medical team quickly whisked him into his incubator after a quick look at him, so he could be fully assessed later on, due to his prematurity. Twin B, yet to be met, remained within. The obstetrician wondered why we were not excited about Twin A, but after hours of labor, epidurals, pain and monitoring, we were both so exhausted. With our deeper knowledge, we prayed that all would be well with Twin B, the child who was in the upper right of the uterus.

The baby would not come down. The contractions continued, and yet there was no movement. Finally, the obstetrician, in a very bold move, inserted his arm in and manually pulled him down into position, pulling his frail little body into the world, the light, and into taking a breath. Twin B, Kenneth Richard, was born. With an APGAR of 2, he was pale and virtually lifeless, and it took the professional's immediate action to get him to finally breathe. The look of both my husband and I confirmed what we had been divinely warned, and we were prepared to meet this new challenge. We were saddened, yet thankful, for the Divine's warning, knowing that this child was "Embraced by the Divine." The reasons, yet unknown, would be revealed.

Torn between two worlds of a healthy baby and the ill baby, it was hard to be both happy and concerned at the same time. That very first night, while Kevin was in NICU for observation, Kenny struggled. And my husband and I slept together in the hospital bed, entwined in hope and fear as I tried to rest and recoup. Giving and receiving support to each other as we awaited the preliminary findings. Our first diagnosis was that of diaphragmatic hernia which, if confirmed, would require immediate surgery with a 50 per cent success rate. Our world crumbled. Margaret graciously performed an emergency baptism, and from that moment on, our son was divinely gifted back to God, "Thy Will is done, on Earth as it is in Heaven." Knowing that the arms of the Divine were truly wrapped around this child, we parents were entrusted into this journey with this precious child.

Four and a half months of journey ensued. We traveled back and forth between the world of home and hospital. We brought Kevin as often as possible to be with his brother Kenny. Returning home to resume the farm and home life of a home with a healthy newborn, we felt torn to be back with our unwell son. Kenny endured IVs, tube feeds, a tracheostomy, blood transfusions, the sterile environment of hospitalization and the technology to maintain his frail little body. It was a time of small triumphs and major setbacks. His frail heart hadn't closed the ventricular shunt that occurs in utero, his lungs were not strong enough to breathe on their own, his deformed aorta was wrapped around his trachea, and there was the shock of the farm accident that had occurred just after his conception. Kenny endured and strived to survive beyond expectations. The love that exists between parent and child strove to overcome the frailties and limitations of the physical realm. Most of all, I remember the look of knowing that passes between parent and child that indelibly links soul to soul.

At four months, when Kenny was at his peak as a lovely baby who was showing the promise of life, we had a beautiful baptism for the twins. With both babies swaddled in satin gowns, despite Kenny's tracheostomy, our families – both our personal families and our medical families – and our beloved priest were granted a beautiful event of this dual baptism in full regalia. Even the head doctor of the PCCU (Pediatric Critical Care Unit) took time to act as photographer for this beautiful and enduring special event of the life of our twins, together.

Three weeks later, with failing health, our son Kenny endured open-heart surgery – the first of several planned for his tiny body – to replace a heart valve and close the hole in his heart. On Thanksgiving Day, 1988, our frail little son endured five hours of touch-and-go surgery before coming back to us in the PCCU for stabilization. We were by his side when he opened his eyes. Eyes that opened with color so blue and bright so as to bless us with a gift of heaven before his tiny struggling heart stopped. I will never forget the glimpse of that gift as the medical team moved into CPR mode, but to no avail. I remember the surgeon opening his chest to manually compress his heart, staff standing by with tears in their eyes, as I finally begged them to stop, and lovingly let him go.

This beautiful, special, divinely gifted child was allowed his peace. His journey, his struggle was over. His little, beautiful life and journey were over. The reason and purpose yet unclear, other than what we thought was his strength of character, and the love that the staff had given him. He showed many that natural desire of life to thrive despite the challenges.

Forever implanted in my heart and in the memory banks of my mind was the vision of the crying nurse who brought our little son to us in the quiet room. We were holding him for the one and only time without tubes, or dressings, or life. Devoid of the life essence, yet he was still our creation of life in our hands. Holding him, cradling him and sharing him with each other, before truly Lovingly Letting Him Go. Into the hands of the Divine – loved, safe, and at peace. His spirit unbroken, yet transcended.

This is where the story could end, and in fact this was not the original story submitted to this book. There is purpose to everything Divine. Kenny's role has been to be a Divine Guide to his brother Kevin. An inspiration to us parents. A continued guide and support as a piece of us living has reached beyond the stars and the heavens and resides with the Divine. The lesson of life, of love and, yes, of loss too, reside in my heart every day. Unending, unyielding. No parent should ever need to bury a child. It is not in the normal scheme of things, nor is it the purpose of conception. But … many do, holding, for a glimmer of time, the hand of their child. "On Eagles' Wings" was the song that my friend, and nurse who was there at the time of his birth, sang at his funeral. It haunts me to this day as to the promise of being lifted up, when my time does come. However, I do know that when we cross, we are just a breath away. Still connected and still loved, just seeing this world and those with whom we are connected with different eyes.

Through the ensuing years, which seem to pass in rapid succession, I have seen the evidence of that still very real and very powerful bond. I have seen it in the twin-to-twin connection of my sons. I have smelt it in the faint scent of baby powder when I am feeling all alone. I see it in the presence of an eagle that passes my line of sight. I also know that a piece of the Divine is with us all, and we are not to think that this is not truth, for its magnificence is never to be doubted. May everyone and everything that crosses your path be blessed with this knowledge. No matter how trivial or inconvenient or difficult, be blessed with this insight. We are all connected here and beyond. Be careful with your words and actions, for the ties that connect transcend the here and now.

Love is forever. Years of grieving marred the gift. Now, with the clarity of time, I know I am touched and truly embraced by the Divine through the gift of my son, Kenny. It was an honor to lovingly let him go, a piece of us, an emissary to the great beyond, the Divine.

Finding my voice and helping others through the sharing of words, wisdom, and the wisdom of others whom I held dear has led to great connections I never expected. Michelle Mayur being one of them! Beautiful, soul-filled connections of love that expand beyond borders and time zones exist.

I have even hosted a telesummit series! Yes! It was a giving back to all those who had filled my cup of life – being able to host them in grateful thanks. I now host a broadcasting network online, allowing a space for others to house their podcasts. I am also in the process of setting up online radio to further broadcast those transformational podcasts in other forms of enlightenment. Hoping and helping those out there, like me, to find the answers their hearts and minds are looking for. Creating community to embrace and know that you can live a life of value, non-judgmentally. I thank Michelle for inviting me into this space, this book and for sharing this piece of my life journey. My hope is that you do not feel alone, no matter what your story is. I do know that what does not serve you is painful, and that lovingly letting it go may open the door to the rest of your life.

Knowing that we are connected to everyone and everything that passes through our life, I acknowledge that not everyone, both living and beyond, is here for our highest best and good. This special Prayer of Release is VERY powerful. I have used this in situations that are holding me back from my goals and dreams. Use this prayer carefully, as the results will sever these connections completely.

RELEASING AGREEMENT PRAYER

I call upon Jesus Christ,

Lord Sananda and Divine Mother

To cancel, release and dissolve,

Any contracts, agreements, commitments,

Exchanges, trades, or relationships

That I may have made at any time

In my multidimensional existence

Which are limiting my Wholeness in any way.

These commitments, contracts, trades

Exchanges, agreements and relationships

Are now dissolved, released, canceled, let go,

Made null and void on every level

Of my multidimensional existence.

In the name and through the power of Jesus Christ,

In the name and in the power of Divine Mother,

In the name and in the power of Lord Sananda,

I know that I am free.

All frameworks, structures, circuitry,

And multidimensional matrices

That have developed as a result

Of these now canceled contracts

Are now dissolved, collapsed, let go,

Released on every level of my energy field now,

And I am opening fully in Wholeness of Divine Love,

Aligning with Wholeness of Divine Truth,

Allowing Wholeness of Divine Grace,

Thank you God, and So It IS.

BRENDA PEARCE (Canada) is an inspired entrepreneur and media presence. She is the CEO of E Factor Live on Demand Media Network, and is a coach, broadcaster, and best-selling co-author. She is also a Registered Nurse and mom to her three beautiful children, and one precious angel son. Some of the ways you can connect with her are on E Factor Radio Network: WWW.EFACTORLIVE.COM and on E Factor Live on Blog Talk Radio HTTP://WWW.BLOGTALKRADIO.COM/EFACTORBRENDAPEARCE

 BRENDA'S FREE GIFT: 5 Days of Distance Reiki Love & Support at HTTP://EMBRACEDBYTHEDIVINE.COM/GET-YOUR-BONUS-GIFTS/

Grieving the Loss of
the Illusion of Myself
– Deb A. Scott

*The seeds to succeeding are unexpectedly
buried in the soil of sincere suffering.*

Was it the death of both my parents within a year of each other, the end of a 20-year medical sales career, the loss of a million dollars, two engagements, friendships that I thought would last forever, or merely the illusion of myself that died?

I have learned to respect loss in a way that I never imagined before God began pruning me away from my attachment to "stuff." The stuff in my head, the stuff in my home, the stuff that I thought defined me. Pruning hurts, but disguised within the appearance of death down to a tiny nub, I learned it is the only way to grow a new life in greater balance, strength and beauty.

I believe the greatest value you can contribute in this life is to create something that will outlast it. Wisdom lasts. I needed to get my God glasses on in order to clearly see the truth of myself before I could begin to imagine the good change I yearned to experience. This is a story of discovering the seeds to succeed are unexpectedly buried in the soil of sincere suffering.

I grew up as an only child in a time when that was not so common. It's hard to believe when I consider my dad was the eldest of six children, and my mom the youngest of five. I think I started multiple rumors that my mom was having another baby just to fit in with the neighborhood kids around town. I didn't want to be different.

Mom was battling her own demons of depression while trying to raise me. I guess it was more than she could handle, because my nana, my mother's mother, came to live with us when I was only six. She stayed with us my whole life, even to the end, finally dying in my arms in the upstairs bedroom at the ripe old age of 94.

I didn't understand what was wrong with my mother, or why the number of years of hell she endured always coincidentally coordinated with the exact number of my age. I did not understand why mom and dad fought all the time, I just remember feeling unloved. What can a child possibly comprehend about mental illness, paying bills, or marriage challenges? No, I just saw things in terms of loving and being loved. In an ironic sort of way, getting older hasn't changed that at all. It truly is all about the love.

I am not sure when I began to consider my home wasn't "normal," but I think I knew it intuitively from the start. It just didn't feel right that I couldn't seem to do anything right for mom and dad. Most of my friends talked at dinner instead of yelled. No one else seemed to be crucified for spilling a glass of milk like me. I was being trained to live an upside-down life of low self-esteem where personal value was dependent on what I did or did not do, and what I won or lost, instead of who I was being in this moment. I was an expert in the school of conditional love at a very early age.

The plot thickened and I ran with open arms into the script of buying the world's material lie.

I'll get good grades, I'll get bad grades. I'll be a class officer, I'll just get stoned. I'll be a cheerleader, I'll run track, and I'll get sexually abused by a teacher. I'll search on the outside for something to make me feel better on the inside.

Counterfeit happiness cost me myself.

It is the realization of this tragic loss that has propelled me into this personal quest to find authentic joy, peace and purpose for myself and all those I meet. That's why I'm writing this story. I hope and pray that you will get the message I wish I could go back in time to tell myself. There is something redemptive in sharing the gift of wisdom with another kindred soul on this short journey we call life.

College held some really great years. A sort of cocoon shielding me from the real world, it was a time of innocence, unconditional love, learning, laughter, confidence and having a whole life ahead of me with an unwritten script of unending possibilities. I truly appreciate the blessing of those years now, much more than I could have ever imagined.

At that time, Regis College in the greater Boston area was a private Catholic all woman's college. Taught by the Sisters of St. Joseph, it was surprising to many I decided to go there, having spent my younger grades in the public school system. Or perhaps it was the perfect subconscious hide-a-way to heal my wounds from all the insanity I had faced growing up. It seemed for the most part the nuns who taught there were more concerned about each of us getting good grades than we were, and they took it as a personal failure if we didn't succeed. Now that is unselfish dedication and commitment I have come to truly respect and admire.

I loved the college swim team, and although I never had any previous competitive swimming experience, as did the other young woman who made the team, I think the coach put me on the team merely out of my enthusiasm and tireless commitment. Hard work did pay off, and being the best swimmer on the team wasn't everything, that was for sure, because I ended up being elected by my peers as co-captain my senior year. Despite being on a competitive college sport, the team members were much more about collaboration than competition, and I learned the quality of caring about others' success more than my own. I grew up.

As a biology major who had laboratory assignments in addition to regular classes, unlike the other majors, I discovered a lot about the value of structure and discipline. I had to work hard to get good grades, and maintained a regular ritual of classes, labs, swim practice, dinner and library to get everything done. Weekends were of course a different story.

I graduated as one of the Who's Who in Colleges and Universities for my class, and a member of Beta Beta Beta, the national biological honor society. I had entered with the intention to become a laboratory medical technologist, and I was departing ready to embark in the world of medical sales. I had big dreams to succeed and show the world what I could do and become. I had no fear, doubts or hesitation. I was ready and had decided the world was ready for me too.

I got a great job offer in Atlanta, Georgia, and although I had never been there, I knew it was time to start packing my bags. My father fought the decision, but my mother encouraged me to take the risk, perhaps out of her own regret or resentment for not pursuing an acting career in California when she was my age. Regardless, they drove down and helped me unpack, get settled, and start a new life.

Now it wasn't all that much being alone, because my navy boyfriend, whom I had met senior year at a welcome dance, was now stationed in Charleston, South Carolina. He drove out to see me just about every weekend when he wasn't at sea, and when you're 22, a five-hour drive each way is like a trip to the local grocery store 25 years later. Oddly enough, we were together for a long while after that, and although we went looking for engagement rings to get married at the seven-year mark of our relationship, we never did make it to the altar. I guess I wasn't ready to settle down and stop enjoying all this attention and success I was enjoying in my career, traveling, making money, searching and seeking for more, more, more. I really believed I had all the time in the world.

While living in Atlanta, I was responsible for the sales in seven southern states: North Carolina, South Carolina, Georgia, Tennessee, Alabama and some of the Florida panhandle, Mississippi and Louisiana. As the first college sale representative the company hired, I made rookie of the year and top in sales my first year. And so the poison of people's jealousy began, like a spoonful of arsenic slowly confusing my perception of myself, I began to realize this wasn't Regis College anymore.

I moved back home, missing my New England roots, proclaiming never to leave the greater Boston area again, only to accept a job in New Haven, Connecticut. The never-ending theme song of sacrificing personal wants for professional gains. It had to be done. The job was everything, career was everything, and success was everything. That is what they told me, and so I told myself.

I sincerely loved that job selling sutures with a Fortune 500 medical device company. I got to be in surgery, build customer relationships, attend travel conventions and work the home office territory. I did very well there, winning my first of many Gold Cups for outstanding sales, and eventually earned a transfer to the Boston territory three years later. Or I should say "fought" for my transfer three years later.

So here is another shocking lesson I learned which I thought would never happen to me. One of those sexist stories I thought people made up. The one where the male national sales director expects you to sleep with him to pay for the job transfer you earned. Yup, that was me. Like a car that hits you from behind without any warning, I really had no idea what was coming. "So how badly do you want that transfer Deb?"

Naivety was a disease I severely suffered from despite my many challenging life events. I think it's a result of that upside-down family boot camp training, the one that neglected proper nurturing, communication and love. My eyes simply did not see, my ears did not hear, and I justified bad behavior at the expense of myself.

I got my transfer to Boston only as a result of my threat to expose the director's behavior. Needless to say, I was no longer the favored employee of this particular individual and, from that day forward, he always looked for a reason to help me leave to keep his little secret safe.

Another lesson I learned the hard way is that people in business and in the business of living can be revengeful. Not necessarily because of anything you have or have not done, but mostly because of what they have done and not done. The world is not fair. When we expect life to be fair we will always lose. Only God is fair. Expectations are pre-meditated resentments. People fail, make mistakes, and are dealing with their own problems and challenges on their life journey.

It seemed the more awards I won, the more competitive everything with management got. It was hard to for me to take orders from a manager who never accomplished as much as I had. The more I sold, the more I had to sell. I could never rest or get ahead of that moving carrot. It was an impossible pace to maintain. After seven years with this company, having built some great relationships with customers and colleagues, I finally moved on and accepted the dream job all my medical sales friends wanted, which turned out to be the ultimate job from hell.

Did I really have to prove myself all over again? Didn't the people in this new company know who I was? I had a hard time swallowing my pride, following their rules, or taking an honest look at my own behavior. My worth was based on other people's opinion of me, never the opinion I had of myself.

And so I found another job, one that I thought was more compatible despite the fact I was going to be the only woman on the entire national sales force. I covered all of New England and Upstate New York. It was a difficult product to sell in conservative New England, but I still won some Ranger of the Year awards they created for the sales person who overcame obstacles. At the end of four years, it became the first and only job from which I was fired. They replaced me with two men. Here is another great lesson: people don't always get fired because of something the person being fired did, but often because of something the manager doing the firing can't do. Remember, Walt Disney was fired from his newspaper job because his manager said he didn't have enough creative ideas.

It was suddenly beginning to dawn on me that there was one constant thread in all these jobs – me! Regardless, I got up, dusted myself off, and started all over again. I got a new job, a better job and my highest paying job. Despite some ups and downs, I really liked that job and the company culture. I had learned some tough lessons though, and I paid attention to my past. I paid attention to my intuition and I began to stop making excuses for bad, unfair and unjust behavior. Despite it all, maybe out of spite, I still won lots more sales awards, all of which collect a lot of dust in my downstairs closet today.

Now at this time in my mid-30s I began to feel something I had never given a moment's thought to before: a biological clock. I suddenly wanted to get married and have a family. The problem was I had spent every waking moment on my career and it suddenly seemed all the good ones were gone. Then along came engagement number two, living in sin, the good-looking guy, who had only been married twice before with three children from these two marriages. I was captivated by those shocking good looks, smooth-talking lies and great sex. Four years of all that drama just about killed me. You know what they say is true: "If it doesn't kill you, it will make you stronger."

I didn't really understand the disease of alcoholism, or that even if an alcoholic does not drink, he/she is still an alcoholic. The lies, the manipulation, the deception, the cheating, they just add another ism to the pile of isms pie. Ending that relationship was like giving up a drug. I went into deep withdrawal and depression that I thought I would never survive. I could barely function.

And so it goes that people don't change because they see the light, they change because they feel the heat. I was burning alive.

At the suggestion of my therapist, I discovered a group called Al-anon, for those who have a loved one or a family member who is an alcoholic. It uses the same 12 steps of Alcoholics Anonymous. I lived for those meetings, and went to them almost daily for years. That free group of anonymous members helped me to heal more than anything else, other than lots and lots of prayer.

I suddenly began to see that in my pointing the finger so quickly at other people for their wrongdoing and bad behavior that three fingers were pointing back at me. I was part of the cause of my own problem. Could I also be part of the solution?

God was growing me. I was discovering a completely new world, and I liked that the value of my existence was no longer hinging on my job, who I was dating, or other people's opinion of me. I was beginning to taste authentic freedom.

When my company sold our division and offered a package to those who opted not to join the new management, I took it without missing a beat. I thought I was going to travel to Europe with my girlfriend, only to discover God had other plans.

Within months after taking that package to fill up my bank account, my mother became very ill. Despite doctors at one hospital telling us it was nothing serious, it certainly didn't look that way from the way she was rapidly losing weight and walking in obvious pain. January 12, 2004 was a difficult day in Massachusetts General Hospital when the surgeon came in to tell us it was cancer. I can honestly say it was one of the few times I ever saw my dad break down in tears like a helpless child.

I knew in that one moment why I got that financial package: to leave my job to be able to take care of my mom (and dad). It was never about a trip to Europe, it was about a trip to heal my soul. It was the longest journey I ever took.

Chemo and radiation became constant companions. My mother and I discovered each other and ourselves on those trips in and out of Boston. We discovered beautiful things we loved about each other in ways we could never have done had it not been for the cancer. Cancer became an unexpected ally.

In the midst of all this my dad became gravely ill again. He had battled death's door many times before, but with my mother failing miserably, he was left with little fight for the war.

Almost one day to the year from her diagnosis, my mom, who had become my best friend in those final 10 years, passed away on February 5, 2005. I never felt pain like that in my life. I remember waking up in the hospital room with her at Mass General at 1:35 a.m. feeling a breeze over my hands when I couldn't hear the sound of her breathing any more. I yelled for the nurse, "I think my mom is dead, I think she's dead!" I was no stranger to death; I had seen it in holding my nana. It had returned with that final echo of emptiness I would never silence. It was the end.

Leaving the empty Mass of Mass General at 2:15 in the morning, I called my dad, and then called a friend, who stayed on the phone with me the whole way home. Life was so unfair.

Being the sole caregiver to my mom was just the start. My dad passed away almost a year after she did on May 4, 2006. He was far from the best friend my mom was, but I still tried to take care of him with the same love and respect as her. We had a small healing in his final three months, and I suppose that was another unexpected gift, as both life and death afford each of us the opportunity to make peace with our past.

I sold my home, moved into the house I grew up in, and cried a lot in isolation, wondering what happened to my life. Where did it go? I was paralyzed by all the stuff I had to go through: 50 years' worth of stuff in the attic, the closets, the desk drawers, and the cellar, everywhere. A survivor of the great depression, my mom never threw anything away.

I was surely not going back to work and fortunately, between my savings and what my parents left me, I was ok. And here comes another great lesson I learned. The same friends who tell you to make sure you invest your money wisely are the same friends who will leave you once you lose it all.

I had researched and invested my $1,000,000 family savings into Millennium Bank for a six percent interest rate with monthly interest income checks being sent to me by the American-based bank, Washington Mutual. Then I learned of someone called Madoff, and something called a Ponzi, and then I saw that the bank where I had put all my money was one of those mentioned on a CNN news report I just happened to catch while at the gym.

Now began the realization of another illusion: that money buys security; that the justice system is designed for justice; that people who claim to love you for who you are might only care about what you have, and what you can give them.

I was getting an intravenous therapy line of an enormous bolus of truth serum. The shattered illusion of the glass house of lies I had bought was like crawling over glass, leaving me a bloody mess. I lamented the loss of my dreams. The one thing about losing it all is that you never have to be afraid of losing it again. But when would it end? How would it end? Where do I go? What do I do?

Life is a process.

I want to tell you there is a happy ending, or at least a happy intermission to this sad story. This is the gift: I enjoy my own company more now than I ever did before. At the brink of burying the illusion of myself, I discovered gratitude for who I have become through it. I look at life differently now, and I hope you will too.

This is what I want you to know, because you are not reading this by accident. God has more wisdom than you and me, and if we let go of what we think we want, God will be able to give us what we need. You're worth the time and effort it takes to discover yourself. Not only for you, but for your husband, wife, children, and every person you meet. The life you live is the message you teach.

I discovered the weeds of control and fear, self-doubt and lack of forgiveness suffocated my ability to believe God exists, and that now I can truly trust He always has my best interest at heart. I can't possibly judge if something has been a good thing or a bad thing in my life while I am still living my life, because I'm not finished yet. God's not finished with me yet. He's not finished with you.

Today I:

1. Take time to nurture my relationship with God first before all others.
2. Take time to pray for myself and others with compassion.
3. Take time to be grateful for everything.
4. Take time to say I'm sorry and thank you each day.
5. Take time to remember: I'm not staying, this is just temporary housing.
6. Take time to listen.
7. Make time to love.

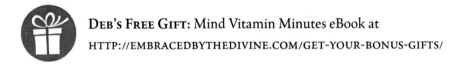

DEB SCOTT, BA, CPC (United States) is a four-time award-winning author of, *The Sky is Green & the Grass is Blue* (**a Kindle Top 20 Best Seller!**), a top-rated best podcaster winner for, The Best People We Know Show, with more than 1 million global listeners, and a Top 1% Kred Social Media Influencer. Deb spent 20 years as a cardiovascular surgical specialist, winning numerous awards for outstanding sales and leadership skills. In her personal life, Deb battled sexual abuse, others' alcoholism, dysfunctional relationships, depression, was the sole caregiver to both her parents who fought cancer to their death, and even experienced financial devastation. Today, Deb helps people turn things around in their business, or the business of living, with the discovery of the amazing you. www.DEBSCOTT.COM

DEB'S FREE GIFT: Mind Vitamin Minutes eBook at
HTTP://EMBRACEDBYTHEDIVINE.COM/GET-YOUR-BONUS-GIFTS/

The Gift of Feeling Intensely
– Julie Ann

We are all being *embraced by the Divine* in every moment of every day. It certainly does not feel like that sometimes, but my own life experience has shown me that this is the truth. I've learned that no matter where we are beginning from, it's possible for each one of us to reconnect with – and feel – the joy, love and guidance that are always flowing to us. To live the life of our dreams, to follow our own heart and to express our true purpose for being alive … while having a lot of fun along the way!

There's a place – *an energetic space* – we can all access. We've all been there from time to time, whether consciously or unconsciously. It's that place where things work out, where synchronicity occurs, where you feel wonderful, where your lucky streak happens, where you feel inspired, where ideas flow, where you meet the right people at the right time. You access this space from *your center*. The core of you, where you are aligned with who you really are. This space of *flow*, of *being in the zone, the vortex!*

It is in this space that the connection with the Divine takes place. Spirit is waiting there patiently, never wavering in its love (which is being beamed to us constantly), for us to meet it there, and we all can.

We are entering a time here on Earth where we can be in this space of connection more and more of the time. We can walk in it and live in it. Not just the gurus in caves, or the healers, or spiritual leaders, or masters or people with "special gifts." All of us.

I know that it may feel difficult, even impossible, to believe. In this rapidly changing world, so many of us are feeling disconnected, overwhelmed, anxious and stressed. Many of us are living "successful" lives and yet we are feeling devoid of purpose and meaning. Many of us are feeling like we are losing "control" – as if the old ways are just not working anymore. Many of us are also feeling that call to step more fully into what we are really here to do, but are maybe not sure of exactly what that is, or are afraid to make that next step.

I understand all of this as I have lived it all. And because of my own journey, and that of my many clients (who have faced challenges ranging from illness to relationship drama to depression), I also know it's possible to come through it all to the other side; to become peaceful, trusting, happy and purposeful. To come to a place where you can not only hear, but follow, the guidance of your heart, which is your connection to your soul, to the Divine.

So let me begin by telling you my own story.

Like many of you I followed the path to "success" and achieved much. I ticked all of the boxes I thought I was "supposed to." Although my childhood was far from easy (I grew up with an alcoholic parent), I did well at school and graduated from University with multiple degrees, culminating in a Masters' Degree in Applied Science. (As a quick aside, my specialty was Artificial Intelligence and that is where I first began to question the nature of consciousness and believe there was "more to it" than the mind alone).

I had a highly paid career working for various research organizations and corporations over the years, and also lectured part-time at University from a very young age. Eventually I set up my own consulting company and worked on a variety of leading-edge projects.

I was generally happy and I enjoyed my work, though I often thought about doing something that was more meaningful, that could really impact people's lives.

I had a close and supportive family who had come through a lot together, and had married quite young to a loving and equally ambitious partner. However I was a chronic worrier … and my "eldest child, overachiever perfectionist" streak would often lead to stress as I tried to "control" situations with my will.

In addition, I was quite shy and often felt uncomfortable in groups or at social occasions. I did feel "different" for some reason that I could never quite put my finger on, and often came away from such events with a sense of uneasiness or discomfort. Almost a knowing of what other people in the group were feeling as a result of the interaction that had just occurred.

However, overall things were good and all continued in this way until my early 30s when a series of events "out of my control" triggered what was lurking below – a massive amount of anxiety just waiting to be unleashed.

I had become aware of this condition in my late 20s when the corporation where I was employed at the time sent my colleagues and me on a "stress management" workshop. The course was great and I just loved the guided relaxation as it was the first time in a long time, if ever, that I had experienced such a feeling of deep peace. What I didn't love was the questionnaire the workshop leader had us complete which showed that although my overall stress levels were a little above average I had an anxiety level above that of 99.9 percent of the population. 99.9 percent … Holy moly!

You can, I am sure, see the irony that receiving feedback like this in a stress management class setting is definitely not good for one's anxiety level!

Anyway, it seemed, in many ways, the fact I was leading a balanced and happy life was keeping the anxiety under wraps (unless I got myself stressed), so rather than deal with the anxiety issue, I just chose to ignore the findings of the workshop questionnaire.

One of the ways the Divine communicates with us is with gentle nudges like this one, which if unacknowledged get stronger and stronger until we are finally forced to take notice. I know that if I had taken action at that point, and dealt with the anxiety issue with meditation or counseling, I would have saved myself a whole lot of drama. Instead, I brushed off this wake-up call and continued snoozing until finally the alarm bells were so loud they could not be ignored any longer.

The series of dramatic life events came one after the other. My beloved Grandma passed away. I took on an incredibly stressful and highly political consulting contract. We were living with relatives while our home was being renovated. Then the straw(s) that broke the camel's back … two miscarriages within a few months of each other.

By the time I had the second miscarriage I was so disconnected from myself that I simply left the hospital after my scan and went straight back to the office (to that highly stressful contract I mentioned above).

In the weeks that followed, the anxiety became all-encompassing, to the point where I remember hardly being able to string two words together into a coherent sentence. I walked around with a knot of tension in my stomach at all times. My nervous energy was out of control. I was totally on edge. But I still didn't realize how far from ok I had become. I was working long hours at a job I hated with no time to think about anything else. Unhappiness and stress can seem so "normal" when you are simply getting through each day, doing what you think you have to, but in fact it's so very far from what our centered, "normal" state really is.

Finally the time came for me to see my obstetrician for a long-avoided checkup post miscarriage and everything caved in. As I sat in her waiting room, no one was more surprised than me when I suddenly started sobbing uncontrollably. I felt like I was hovering above, observing a character in one of those B grade movies. In my head I was thinking, "What on earth is going on? I don't do things like this. I am really together. Look at me – I am successful, I have a nice suit on." Waaah…

My doctor gently told me she thought it would be a good idea for me to get counseling before trying for a baby again. I nodded, sobbing wildly but in my head there it was again: "Me? Don't be ridiculous. This is just a little thing I am having here. Counseling? What would everyone say? I don't think so!"

Maybe you will relate to this when I tell you that I come from a lineage of women who COPE. You know, the stoic ones. Brilliant, strong, heroic "Copers." Admitting to not coping was certainly not something I felt comfortable about back then.

However this letting go of control, the culmination of something that I can now see was something akin to a nervous breakdown, became instead the beginning of a spiritual breakthrough.

I might easily have ignored my obstetrician's advice if it hadn't been for the synchronicity that my long time GP "just happened" to have begun to follow his true calling and was now offering counseling and hypnotherapy as well. He was a very spiritual man, director of a charitable organization (which again "just happened" to teach meditation courses) and very much on his own path. I realize more and more how lucky I was to have had his influence at that time … but then there are no accidents. The Divine does work in mysterious ways after all.

While attending a follow-up medical appointment with my GP, I plucked up my courage and said to him, "I think I am going to come and see you for one of your *other* appointments." When he smiled at me and said, "That's wonderful. I have always known you would come to see me one day." I was very surprised because I really thought I was putting on a pretty good show of keeping it all together. I asked my doctor how he had known I needed help. "Because I see myself in you," he said. "Why do you think I began to do this work? Because I was once where you are now."

It gave me such hope to hear – from this calm, wise man doing such meaningful work – that he had once felt this way. I often think of that reply because years later it was the exact same thing I was able to say to my own clients. And I can say with confidence to anyone who is reading this now, and resonating with the information, that you truly can come through to the other side. And not just survive … but thrive! And that it's nowhere near as difficult as it might seem right now.

I began my counseling and hypnotherapy sessions and started to meditate (something I had been "meaning to do" for the longest time). The anxiety, which most probably stemmed from a feeling of uncertainty in my childhood, began to dissipate.

After a short time my sessions ended, but the meditation continued. I am so grateful that my wonderful doctor not only helped me, but also sent me off on my way with tools to move forward so that I could be empowered on my own journey.

This commitment to a regular personal practice of meditation (and/or other centering techniques I have learned as the years have gone by), I have carried with me to this day. I personally believe this (joyful) commitment is the key to thriving in these changing times, as I'll explain later.

That time in my life changed everything for me. People who have met me since then would be really surprised to hear that I was ever anxious, as I am generally one of the most happy and tranquil people you could meet.

Stress left my life and has rarely returned. I felt truly happy to the core. In patches at first, and then more often. I did not realize I had forgotten what happiness actually felt like, and can remember so clearly the first time it spontaneously showed up. It was a simple moment of driving somewhere with the sun streaming into the car. I can still remember how good it felt, and with that a moment of awareness of feeling something that I had not felt for the longest time. What I now recognize as the feeling of connection and wholeness.

And yes ... I got pregnant, twice within two years. I now have two amazing teenagers and one thing I know FOR SURE is that these beautiful beings could not have come to me in the state I was in.

So looking back now I can only be grateful I went through that experience because unbeknown to me at the time, it opened up my spiritual path and was the beginning of a new phase of awareness and of life.

A huge gift of that time was an understanding that the ability to feel emotions so intensely was actually a blessing. As I became more in touch with my own core and emotions, I began to realize that the anxiety was also due to an extreme sensitivity to energy. I came to see that I was highly empathic and often sensed other people's emotions/vibrations. When we are not centered and in control of our own vibration we are much more affected by the energy of others, which is why I often felt uncomfortable in large groups. But when we spend more and more time aligned with our own core, these sensations, like the one anxiety brings, are invaluable guidance and an intuitive gift.

If you had asked me before this experience if I had any psychic gifts or abilities I would have said, "No." In my mind back then, those gifts were limited to clairvoyants or channels. Special people who could *see* visions and *hear* messages from the Divine. I believed that others had those abilities, but I myself had never actually seen an angel, or had a psychic vision or heard a revelation from above.

As it turns out, however, sensitivity to energy is in fact a wonderful intuitive gift known as clairsentience and a powerful tool once we learn how to channel it. And this blessing, which was once a huge challenge, has been a major component in my work as a healer and teacher.

I am sure many who are reading this have this gift also, and in fact we are all intuitive and all of us, every single one of us, receives guidance via emotion, as our positive and negative feelings show us when we are *on track* and close to our *center*, or not. In fact, if you are currently experiencing anxiety or depression there is a good chance that this could be due to spiritual gifts which you are unaware of, or may even be suppressing. Energy healing would be highly beneficial for you, as would a commitment to your own daily practice.

This practice of centering, which I'll talk about below, is becoming more and more important in these changing times because as you may be aware, the Earth is receiving wave upon wave of powerful energy in the form of solar flares and astrological alignments. And those who are sensitive (including many children) are feeling this acutely. This is a good thing, as these waves are bringing light to awaken and transform our world, but if you are not centered, you can be emotionally thrown around like a leaf in the wind by these energies. If you are in alignment with your core, however, the solar energy can enhance your own feelings of wellbeing and bliss.

Which leads me to talk about the other major blessing of that time (around 20 years ago now) which was learning a system of meditation. When I began to meditate, I had no idea of the impact this daily ritual of connection was to have on my life. I did not begin it for spiritual reasons. I did it to relieve stress and to feel more peace and relaxation, as many of us do. The very process of meditation, by distracting us from resistant thought, brings us back to *our center*, the space of connection I mentioned earlier.

There are other techniques that can also move us towards and into that space. Breathwork, guided visualization, self-healing, gratitude journaling or any of the other wonderful suggestions given by the authors here, including the powerful exercise I've included below.

Most of us already know of, or have learned some of these techniques, but the magic only happens when we practice, when we experience and feel often. So I really recommend finding a way that works for you and committing to it.

The more we practice, the more we find ourselves naturally carrying this energy into our everyday lives.

In addition, via the powerful Universal Law of Attraction, through which *like attracts like,* we attract more of what we put out into the world. The energy we radiate draws to us the events, things, thoughts, visions, ideas and people that match its vibration or essence. For those of us who have always loved to be *in control*, this is where the true control and power lies. Because, as we choose to radiate a different energy, we gracefully and easily create change around us; a change that comes from within.

As we live more and more from our center, in this space of connection, our path begins to unfold in a way that is more aligned with what we could call *Divine Will.* This is our own personal purpose and part of the Divine Plan (and what will bring us the most joy and meaning in this lifetime).

From this space, we are also more able to feel and hear our guidance, and this ability to have such clarity and focus in the over-stimulated world we live in is almost like a superpower!

We are also able to parent more effectively and be a stabilizing influence for our children, many of whom are also highly sensitive to energy as mentioned previously.

So a daily practice was life changing for me (and I know it can be for you) and my journey evolved from there ... quite slowly at first, and then very rapidly.

When my children were still very young I moved countries and stepped into my spiritual work. The move into healing and teaching seemed to come out of the blue, but that's a whole other story. Let's just say that all of the elements *fell into place* and the pathway opened before me and continues to evolve.

That's not to say there have not been challenges along the way. The path is not a straight one, and there may be lessons to be learned, but one advantage of being *in the center* for at least some of the time is that you are more easily able to see the blessings in the lessons and to trust that some changes are truly for the best.

Having said that, I am now so blessed to be closer every day to living my true version of success, which is to be free to follow my heart and make decisions based on the calling of my soul. In other words, *to follow my bliss.* I've had the most incredible and magical experiences and I know there are many more to come.

And for you as well. When YOU are really ready to follow your own path these are the steps I would suggest:

The most important first step, I believe, is to consciously take responsibility for your own life and healing. We've all of us had challenging events in our lives, sometimes when we were children (which can seem so unfair), but we really cannot truly move forward until we let go of the victim mentality and stop blaming others. Remember you are doing this for yourself.

Ask for help if and when you need it. Find healers or teachers who resonate, but don't give your power away by thinking they will do the healing for you. Real change must come from within.

Commit to making time for yourself every day to do that centering and reconnecting. As little as 15 to 30 minutes a day will benefit you. First thing in the morning is perfect because it sets your energy for the day. For many women this commitment to themselves is the part they find most difficult. Many of us put everyone else's needs first, but that old chestnut about putting your own oxygen mask on first really does apply here. If you are sensitive to energy, this commitment is even more important.

This time you commit to each day paradoxically creates MORE time for you. That's the beauty of this state of flow and connection. In this space, the Divine takes care of many of the details for you.

Believe that this doesn't have to be hard. Due to the shift that is taking place on the planet, and the work done by many energy workers, including the contributors to this book, it is much easier than ever before to move into and hold this space of connection. There is no need for years of study and suffering. Start the process today, be committed, and you will reap benefits very quickly.

If you want to know what I believe is the easiest way to shift into the space of connection: it's simply gratitude. I've come to experience gratitude/appreciation as one of the most powerful and transformative energies on the planet. And this energy is available to each and every one of us in every moment. I'm not talking about the kind of gratitude we feel we "owe" someone in return for something they have done for us, but gratitude as a way of seeing the world through different eyes. Make a choice to look for the good in every situation.

Due to the powerful Law of Attraction discussed earlier, when you truly FEEL gratitude, when you radiate it out into the world, you attract more and more to be grateful FOR. When you view your life with appreciation, you are experiencing a form of unconditional love, which is truly divine. As the world changes, so much is now possible for us … things beyond our wildest dreams and beyond what we can imagine. Gratitude opens us up to this limitlessness and allows the Divine to bring your path and purpose to you. This must truly be *felt* to be believed.

So here's a powerful little visualization you can do daily as a centering exercise. It's based around the energy of gratitude and will help draw to you events, thoughts, inspirations and ideas to move you forward on your path.

I hope you enjoy it, and if you would like more information about this gratitude process and the Law of Attraction, and a free recording of this meditation please see the "FREE Gifts and Resources from the Author and Collaborators" page at the end of this book.

Centering Meditation

Begin by breathing deeply, down into your abdomen.

With every inhalation, say the words THANK YOU (in your mind).

With every exhalation, let go of everything you need to release....

Repeat for as long as you wish.

Then when you are ready

IMAGINE yourself at some time in the future, standing on top of a mountain, or in a very special place you love.

You are standing, with your arms raised to the sky, saying "THANK YOU, THANK YOU, THANK YOU!" to the Universe for all that has come to you. More than you could have ever dreamed of.

You are FEELING so grateful.

Let that feeling of GRATITUDE move into every cell in your body, and feel it radiate out from you. Enjoy the feeling. Stay there a while. Smile.

Now bring your focus back to the present and focus on all that you have to be grateful for NOW. There is SO much to be grateful for.

Whenever you are ready, open your eyes.

Go about your day carrying this beautiful feeling of gratitude with you.

Do this daily and EXPECT wonderful things to happen. And they will!

JULIE ANN (Singapore) is an Intuitive Healer, Spiritual Coach, Workshop Facilitator, Creator of the "Seeing 11:11 – A Global Vision" daily intention project, and Author of the forthcoming book, *If You Are Looking for a Sign, This Is It!* Julie has facilitated workshops in Malaysia, Philippines, China and Australia as well as her home base of Singapore. She has created several online global intention projects and hosted events during various worldwide meditation gatherings. WWW.JULIEANN.CO

 JULIE ANN'S FREE GIFT: Time for You – eBook and Meditation at HTTP://EMBRACEDBYTHEDIVINE.COM/GET-YOUR-BONUS-GIFTS/

A Life in Metamorphosis
– Raeline Brady

I Came in This Way

As a child my psychic and intuitive gifts were already naturally developed, particularly clairaudience and clairvoyance, which were especially heightened whilst in nature. Nature spirits revealed themselves to me. As soon as I could talk I was making predictions, e.g. when people were on their way to visit. They would show up on our doorstep unannounced not long after. Once, at the local fair, I told my Mum that our relatives were looking for us. "Oh no, they live miles away. They aren't here," she said. But our relatives, told of our whereabouts by neighbors, soon found us.

Another time, driving along the Great Ocean Road on a family trip, I excitedly called out from the back seat, "We've been here before, haven't we?" My parents answered, "No, this is a new place." Then I described in detail the scene ahead that was not yet in view. I was then four years old and was soon dubbed the "little witch."

My father was my world. He introduced me to the stars and shared his love of nature and flora. I felt totally safe around him, yet at the same time, like a fish out of water in this world, quickly realizing that what I was experiencing was not the norm. When I was 12 I suddenly experienced great loss when my dad and uncle were both killed in a car accident. It was as if my only safety net had been ripped out from under me. My aunt wrote me a letter of condolence, explaining the various planes of existence and the eternal nature of the soul. Its content was not a revelation, but a relief. Finally, confirmation! I was not the only one in this world aware of other realms of existence and the beings therein.

My psychic abilities increased significantly during this time. I was very young, ill-equipped and petrified of the increase in extrasensory experiences, especially being visited by those who had passed over from this world. I remember crying myself to sleep at night, whilst someone gently stroked my leg. So arrived the initial catalyst for exploring myself and my "other worldly" nature and gifts more deeply.

I continued to struggle with grief and separation over the loss of my father and often thought about death and checking out. I found myself drifting towards what I now call my *Underworld Initiations*. I experimented with a decadent, life-on-the-edge existence. I soon entered the world of Bacchus – sex, drugs and Rock and Roll: socializing, traveling with, and privy to the inner sanctum of some of the most famous and infamous people on the planet, with all the illusory trappings that go with that life. Each took me in, recognizing something in me that I was yet to discover for myself. I was teetering daily on a razor's edge of life and death. Yet, while most were experimenting with various forms of intoxications to "open up" to other realities, I was seeking by the same means to shut it all down!

I was bizarrely on a psychological and emotional rollercoaster ride; one day living in total luxury – caviar, champagne, a jet-set life style – and then literally in the gutter, totally penniless, queuing up at soup kitchens with the so-called "dregs of society." I constantly seesawed back and forth from one reality to another, and observed many people struggling with themselves. I soon learned that it doesn't matter how much money, fame, or glory you acquire or lose; if you do not have a spiritual anchor, you are totally lost in this world. During this phase I witnessed many acquaintances dying and personally experienced three Near Death Experiences – blue-faced, purple-lipped and cold on the floor. Others, less fortunate, didn't survive.

I went through tremendous pain emotionally regarding survivor guilt after experiencing being held at gunpoint with a friend in a robbery attempt. We managed to come out unscathed, but later she went home, self-medicated to calm her nerves, slipped into unconsciousness and drowned in the bath.

Soon after, I underwent a cold turkey experience with a twist, which flung me into my dark night of the soul – days of deliriously writhing in excruciating pain, crying and screaming out in an aggrieved discourse with the Divine. Finally my anger gave way to deep-seated grief. At last

I had an avenue for purging, and purge I did. In a lucid state I remember screaming at God, "Why are you taking all these good people and leaving me here?" And then it all began to turn around.

Through each death experience, I was encouraged to go deeper, but now my own psychic death experience was forcing me to change on all levels and as the intensity grew, the real enquiring began – "Who am I? What am I doing here? What is my relationship with the Divine?" As they say, "Ask the right questions and you'll get the right answers."

Stepping Off

I had learned to see death as an old familiar friend, one that no matter how I tried was not going away. I finally got off the Rock and Roll rollercoaster and graduated the school of hard knocks. When I accepted the good, the bad, the ugly and the beautiful within, there was no returning to being in the dark about myself, my world, and my relationship with The Divine.

With newfound consciousness, I finally recognized that these experiences were crucial ingredients to help me obtain and translate my soul contract for this lifetime. Through rehabilitation, private and group therapy, I soon realized that understanding my psychology, though an important step, was not enough. Suddenly everything in this regard became easy, which was miraculous in itself. It was as if I was suddenly wrapped in a protective shield, all obstacles were removed. Things were unlocking in my body and my cells, my psychic gifts were returning, indeed were ramping up. Lessons in what operates beyond the physical provided the springboard to launch myself into new realms of understanding.

I received Reiki healings and took flower essence remedies and my physical, emotional and mental bodies responded brilliantly. As each block and fear dissolved, I started to re-open my subtle senses and began to take a leap of faith and was not shutting these experiences down. I was guided to share messages with those whose friends and relatives had crossed over. Although I had no real knowledge of the subject, I began relaying messages from a subtle healing team, offering diagnoses of physical and emotional imbalances, plus the appropriate natural remedy, crystal, or modality to quickly restore balance. I was way too open, so this would come anywhere at any time.

Soon after I was at a restaurant and was introduced to the owner after my friend mentioned my gifts as an intuitive healer. He asked if I believed in life after death. I replied, "Yes, of course." He later returned and sat with us to chat. Immediately I saw two male spirits standing behind him. They introduced themselves as Peter and Robert and said to relay that they were well, happy and working in a beautiful garden, and not to worry about them. He smiled and said, "Thank you. My father and brother were recently killed in a car accident, and their names are Peter and Robert."

Although overwhelming at times, I realized this ability was bigger than me and brought comfort and relief to those in need – and no matter how I tried, it was not going away. And so the theme of death and transformation continued. Each death experience would bring on another initiation. This time it was surrender. I chose to see these abilities, and this life, as gifts not curses. But, to sustain that, I first had to learn to adjust my aperture. I decided to learn Reiki, which immediately restructured my channel to become attuned, rather than bombarded with frequencies. At last I had acquired the vibrational stabilizer to feel secure.

My spirit guides and guardian angels, each in turn, became my closest allies and wisest teachers, providing wisdom and knowledge of the Earth's energy lines and celestial portals. Although very personal, I was encouraged to share this information with others. Yet every time I did, my palms would sweat, I had palpitations and I would shake uncontrollably. I had come too far and experienced too much to shut it all down again. I realized I had no choice but to trust this wisdom, and my soul directives, and to take the leap of faith. I started to write and share wisdom through a meditation group. I had my own clinic, students and clients and, although satisfied with my life, I had itchy feet. I felt I must reach more people, to share my experiences and get my brand of what I was doing out to the world.

Holy Cow

Suddenly I was directed by my guidance to go to all the places where I had energetically opened up and fed song-lines, and place holy water from the Ganges at each site. Things moved quickly! Six weeks later, I was living on the banks of the Ganges in India, in Mayapur, a holy city on a powerful Earth grid line, where the river Ganges crosses the Tropic of Cancer.

Before I could drop off my bags, I was whisked off to the cow shed, to see a small calf writhing in agony. My hostess hoped my Reiki skills could help. His mother was screaming out to him. Anthrax had gripped him; he lay in the final stages of death. I knew it was too late. When this became apparent the women sprang into action. I was shown right then and there how to assist souls in leaving the material world; a process that is truly humbling and still today amazes me to be part of. I would later marvel that, whether in animal or human body, the phenomenon of the soul departing the Earth realm is the same for all beings – and not always easy, due to material attachments. So in this way, my soul calling of working with natural death cycles naturally emerged.

Clearly a hospice was necessary. Over the next few days a small team was established to counteract neglect. Male calves, especially, fell ill, as they had no monetary value compared with milk-producing females. I looked after a sick young bullock that told me, via Reiki, that his name was Dharma, and shared his story along with other words of wisdom. I hadn't known the beautiful story associated with this name – the qualities of Dharma being represented by a bull. There is no higher dharma than helping others, thinking about the welfare of others, and serving humanity. In the story the bull's front legs are broken as the planet becomes more degraded.

Word got out that I was communicating with cows. The temple authorities ridiculed me. Thus began my next initiation – *Persecution Wounds*. Next morning, figurines of a cow and baby calf on the altar mysteriously fell off, breaking both animals' front legs. This omen created a change of heart towards me, and more importantly a turn-around in regard to the protection of cows.

On the eve of my return to Australia, I awoke, hearing a voice so compelling that I complied: "You are not going anywhere." Instead of the airport, I went to the airline office. They said it was unlikely they would be able to extend the ticket, but would try. Three days later I received a fax: "We regret to inform you we cannot extend your ticket for three months as requested, but can only offer an extension of one year." Yet again, I had to first let go to receive.

In many lifetimes some of us may have experienced ridicule, being burnt at the stake, having the tongue cut out, and even Inquisition for speaking what we know. Sometimes these experiences are so strong in our psyche, we attract those who will best assist in the release. When the wound is great, some even become their own judge and jury, blocking their magical gifts themselves. The valuable lesson of persecution wounds was to release the need to prove or defend what I know, share or experience as my reality. This next initiation provided a dramatic shift in awareness and gave me new freedom in sharing wisdom from the heart to greater audiences.

As destiny would have it, the local authorities decided that if I were to remain I would be given a legitimate job, so as not to be put on the witch-hunt again. When I heard the job description, I nearly fell over. I became a priestess for the temple of Ganga Devi, goddess of the Ganges River. Every five minutes I would lead groups of up to 50 people through flower, incense and prayer offerings, glorifying her divine qualities. Sometimes up to 1,000 people a day attended.

Ancient Sentinels

In India I met Chey, a celibate monk living in India for 12 years. He attended my healing workshop. I was over relationships, and he was never going there. We were thrown together at catapult speed, and so the cosmic joke on us began. We received visions and messages regarding nature through dreams, each holding the missing part for the other. Eventually we married.

Chey was born in Poland, growing up surrounded by magnificent forests and lakes. Often he would sneak out at night to sleep on the forest floor. As fate would have it, we received word that his mother had been misdiagnosed and was in the advanced stages of cancer, so we quickly moved to Poland. Once again my relationship with death was being tested and deepened.

My refuge in all this was the forest and the knowledge we had learned in India, which provided us with the appropriate skills in supporting her through the process of transmigration of the soul.

I soon discovered that the local forests were powerfully ancient and pristine. What followed would change my life path forever. A complete system of vibrational essences called Soul Quintessence System soon arose, which in turn evolved into co-creating vibrational essences at sacred power sites all around the world, from flora on top of sacred mountains, stones at the Pyramids of Giza, from dolphins singing, in crop circles and from healing vines in The Amazon.

Oceanic Consciousness

For many years I conducted seminars, personal consultations and teacher training in many cities around the world. Though satisfied, I still felt there was more.

Again my life took a dramatic turn. I suddenly became gravely ill with double pneumonia and pleurisy, the day the Tsunami of 2004 hit. I had recurring dreams of babies who had drowned coming to me to be sent to their next place of learning. I was releasing ancient grief around earthquake and tsunami scenarios and knew it was a very personal, yet collective, release.

I love the ocean and swimming in it, but could never put my head under water and often became panic-stricken when doing so. Recurring tsunami dreams plagued me; I would wake up in a sweat and became claustrophobic when watching films of this nature. I soon realized that I had to release past life trauma around inundations, and clear catastrophobia from my cellular memory, in order to proceed to the next level of my soul mission. I began asking for guidance and directives and, yet again, an extraordinary initiation was instigated.

I remained bedridden for four weeks, my hands and feet on fire, receiving download after download of information. I began writing, all the while having the strangest sensations of being here, yet simultaneously in an oceanic existence. I soon emerged from my watery rebirth with new consciousness, body, cells and role.

With ancient knowledge, directives, and the required scuba training in hand, I jumped into the abyss! Fully submerged in the oceanic underbelly of Gaia, I began traveling to specific sites around the planet: The Bahamas, Florida Keys, Egypt, Yucatan, Brazil, Galapagos Islands, Bali, Australia, and Hawaii, re-spinning the dormant and warped vortices of the primeval grid via scuba diving. I was flooded with fear, yet compelled to proceed. Directives soon followed regarding an oceanic healing system involving whales and dolphins for the vibrational uplifting of humanity and the Earth, which I in turn pass on to others during retreat workshops, with dolphins involved, at the heart center of The Bermuda Triangle and "The Gateway to The Bahamas," Bimini. Incredible healing, activation, and intimate exchanges occur with our ocean tribes when this is put into action. There is no turning back and this has been my focus ever since.

Since 1991 I have been on a fascinating and inspiring voyage of awakening. Though all our journeys are individually experienced, they may be intricately shared. Thanks for allowing me to share a part with you.

Here Is What I Learned

The series of trials and tests I underwent were a necessary part of the training. Instead of feeling ashamed of my school of hard knocks phase, I came to appreciate it as an apprenticeship that has served me well. When clients and students say others wouldn't understand what they have endured or experienced, I simply share my story. All our experiences are valid and may be a powerful support to others in their journey; always share what has brought you to be who you are today.

I came to realize that when we are in the dark about the unconscious and subconscious parts of Self, and the beings overseeing those yet-to-be-awakened states of awareness, the ignorant, unconscious, ego-fuelled parts run riot and are therefore subject to lessons that only our guides and guardian angels can deliver. When I let go of being perfect and set out to be authentically me, the good, the bad, the ugly and the beautiful parts of Self became meaningful.

No one is ever truly forsaken. If we can't learn the nice way (when avoiding the reclamation of our innate sacred power, wisdom and knowledge as soul contracts for this lifetime), there is always a guardian angel, and even our own True Self, ready to step in and override with whatever it takes. This is very reassuring.

In my experience, there are vital initiations a spiritual aspirant may undergo to quicken spiritual advancement, such as dark night of the soul, deep enquiry, surrender, release of persecutions wounds and clearing "catastrophobia" from the cellular memory.

When these were addressed, they revealed valuable insights regarding the false identities and roles I had become attached to, or believed were the total sum of me, the real me. Such identifications are simply designations that can liberate or entrap us. In the proper context, unconscious mind, faulty intelligence and false ego have provided important shadow self-awareness that continues to bring all facets into alignment with soul awareness and the soul path.

Each near death, grief, pain, acute illness and death experience brought many dangerous challenges and trials that were completely life changing. The cure was oftentimes held in the mystical rather than the mundane, and provided powerful initiatory processes that sequentially spring-boarded me into greater awareness of Self. Each initiation paved the way for a powerful metamorphosis, presented catalysts and provided inspiration for delivering consciousness tools to others, and especially mapped out my specific roles and service to humanity and the Earth.

True Self Exercises

Neither negative nor positive energies require change, but our judgment and projections do. Through integrational awareness, the constraints of the duality reality and polarity pull release their hold. As each situation in life is integrated, a new launch pad for alchemy and transformation can be offered. It is not Earth time that dictates change, but where we choose to place our consciousness at any given moment, and the use of our free will in union with Divine Will. Here is a technique that is simple, yet profoundly useful.

TRUE SELF INTEGRATION
1. Place hands in integration mudra – (hands clasped).
2. Feel for True Self point on body (sternum) with thumbs, whilst hands remain clasped.
3. Speak aloud, "I ask that all that I AM throughout all dimensions, all time and all space integrate and have union with my True Self.
4. I ask that my True Self has union with The Divine; I ask that The Divine has union with my True Self.
5. I ask that my True Self has union with all that I AM." Allow any thoughts, feelings and visions to naturally arise. Visualize any blocks in your body dissolving. Let each issue integrate through a connection with your True Self in union with The Divine. Continue till you feel your energy is clear and flowing.

INTEGRATING SITUATIONS AND PLACES THROUGH TRUE SELF
1. State: "I ask that my True Self in union with The Divine do what is required with this situation or place, [describe here the situation or place] the source of this situation and or place [speak here the situation or place again] and everything connected with this

situation or place. I ask this as a recognized portion of The Divine and an integrated part of the Whole.

2. I ask that my True Self in union with The Divine and The Divine in union with my True Self does what is required to clear and release all links and attachments, integrate and seal all gaps regarding this situation or place." [Allow any thoughts, feelings and or energy blocks in your body to rise and integrate one by one. Continue until you feel your energy is clear and flowing.]

As a dedicated Earth Worker and Gaian Midwife, RAELINE BRADY (Australia) travels the world lecturing, teaching consciousness tools and facilitating retreat workshops to sacred power sites and with dolphins and whales. She is a vibrational essence developer and writer. Raeline is a Master Teacher of Usui, Tibetan and Karuna Reiki, Seichim / Sekhem and her own healing system Radiance Force. WWW.SOUL-QUINTESSENCE.COM Receive complimentary light language activations, empowering star elder wisdom and guided visualizations by following the Soul Quintessence Page on Facebook.

 RAELINE'S FREE GIFT: 10% discounts on selected Soul Quintessence products and services at

HTTP://EMBRACEDBYTHEDIVINE.COM/GET-YOUR-BONUS-GIFTS/

Survive to Soar – Becoming a Financial Phoenix

– Helaine Z. Harris

It was 2007 and I felt as though I was walking in Grace, as my life was the experience of Divine Order.

Everything seemed to be blessed in my life. Even when things didn't work out the way I wanted, they wound up being for the best. I knew it and could feel it. Spirit was with me and I was in the delightful flow of life force energy. That lasted about nine months.

My healing practice was successful. I had plenty of clients and many referrals. Once a year I participated in an expo that brought in enough new clients interested in my expertise to keep me very comfortable. I had a substantial bank account and began exploring investments.

That lasted about nine months.

My Fall from Grace

By 2008, I explored a company that offered several types of training classes and large group meetings with lots of information pertaining to real estate investments. What they were offering were investment properties for very little money down, and they went into depth about how to make it all work out for you. There were a number of people I met who had even purchased five to 10 properties. That was amazing to me since they didn't have the financial foundation to support many properties, so I thought.

At that point in my life, I realized I was getting older and needed to prepare more financially for my future. I had hip replacement surgery a year or two prior to that time and my mind kept telling me to invest some of my money to have it work for me so I could eventually retire. I took classes, went to meetings and ran into several people I knew from other groups and networking events.

The company's main office was in Orange County, California. After checking with the Better Business Bureau and confirming the company had an A rating then, I concluded that this had good investment potential and began checking out properties to possibly purchase. A great opportunity presented itself to me to join a group of about 20 people that this company put together. We all took a bus to Phoenix to check out properties.

We looked at many homes, which were usually two or three bedrooms, some four bedrooms, all in different locations. It was amazing to see people scrambling to purchase one, two or even three properties! They couldn't buy them fast enough.

I kept having this uneasy feeling in my body and my stomach was knotted and uncomfortable. I told myself I was being silly. All these people couldn't be wrong. I got the message in some form that this may not be wise for me, but pushed that inner voice away and bought one property – I was just swept up in that frenzied energy.

After telling the agency handling the rental that I wanted to know the names of the potential tenants (because I am very intuitive), they ignored my request and it was rented without my approval. That was the first sign of problems to come. It had been rented to a family and I was relieved for the time being, although my inner knowing felt there might be issues ahead.

A few other things were going on in my life at the time, which were probably connected to the kind of decision I made on that fateful day. Consequently, I didn't feel in the flow of life force energy the way I did before. My best friend of many years decided to move back to upstate New York because she was unhappy at her job here in the Los Angeles area. One of my daughters was separating from her husband. I was very concerned how she would manage and what she would do. Both of those issues affected me a great deal. I was worried constantly about these situations, which knocked me off my spiritual foundation.

Also, I wound up needing rotator cuff and bicep repair surgery. This meant I was out of commission for a while. Now I was not only spiritually off; I was physically off as well.

Into the Financial Pit of Hell

Then the real problems with the tenants began. They didn't take care of the house and I had to pay fines because of them. After a while, they even stopped paying rent. The excuse they gave was about medical issues, but the mortgage still had to be paid. Guess who paid it? They finally skipped town and the damage they did to the house was very costly. Just what I needed, another huge expense!

The real estate market was one of the main reasons the economy tanked. So many people were purchasing investment properties without enough financial backing. Tragically, the housing market collapsed.

In a three or four-month period in 2009, many of my clients or their partners lost their jobs or had to fold their businesses. That really hit me – my income rapidly halved. I thought it would rise again soon; it always had for me in the past. Instead, I watched my bank account rapidly dwindle. I began using my retirement money to live on.

Eventually I lost the Phoenix property. I could no longer handle two mortgages without a tenant paying rent, as well as a 50 percent loss of income. The mortgage company sold my property at a short sale and I hit rock bottom financially. Now my credit rating, which I had always prided myself on, was destroyed as well.

Abandoned by God

I felt abandoned by God. "Why? I've done so much work on me. I've changed me in so many ways. I've become softer, more loving, and much more compassionate, what else do I need to do? Spirit, so how come you didn't help me figure things out better?" Clearly, I made some very unwise decisions. Of course, it was because I went against Spirit and my inner knowing.

I kept asking myself, "Why is all this necessary? I had already gone through my dark night of the soul a number of years ago. What's this? A *dark time* of the soul, not just a dark night? Come on. That's not right. What about all my 30 odd years of consistent work on myself? Wasn't that enough? Don't I get to rest, ever?"

I felt as though I was on a roller coaster of emotions: shame, fear, anger, sadness, hurt, embarrassment, humiliation, guilt and feeling stupid … really, really, stupid. I became frightened I would lose the house I lived in.

I remembered my intuitive knowing that the Arizona property was not wise for me to purchase, but I ignored it … and paid a huge price for not trusting myself. Yes, I knew the importance of listening to Inner Guidance, but my anxiety about aging took over and I bought a property, denying my own sense of FEAR. That huge downfall. That is what made me make such a grandiose error of judgment! Yes, eventually, I figured it out.

I was so humiliated about what happened that I stopped talking to many of my friends at the time. The shame, the guilt for being so stupid and the embarrassment was too much for me. I was beating myself up; I certainly couldn't deal with anyone else's judgment.

For an extrovert like me to stay away from people was pretty strange. It made me feel even more alone. It was torturous, but when I felt like this, being with people was even worse. I just wanted to hide. Where did my brains go? For someone so smart, I sure did a dumb thing … or so I kept telling myself.

I really spiraled downhill. Things got darker and darker. I had no idea how I would ever come out of this abyss.

So I did what I do best when in a crisis. I began praying and searching for a way out of this dark hole.

The anxiety made it difficult for me to sleep. Instead of sleeping, I kept searching for answers and to find what I needed to do to recover. I read. I tried things. Some things worked, others did not.

I went inside and worked with all those negative lower level emotions that were driving me nuts. I knew that when I was fully on my path and flowing with Source energy, everything worked out. But I was off in a huge way.

Of course, I not only judged myself for screwing up royally, but also for not being spiritual enough to stay in the flow of life force energy.

Working with my shaman medicine teacher helped me to release the terror, shame, anger and humiliation. Every time I wanted to work on my money issue, in addition to releasing my emotions, he would say to me, "Just go into your heart and feel love. Feel the group loving you." I told him that love would not pay my bills. I could barely pay him now.

A realization hit me that I didn't have any new business skills. They weren't necessary before. I was comfortable with my practice, had plenty of clients, even a waiting list at times. I didn't think I even needed a website. Now it seemed like I required all kinds of things I didn't know or have.

One coach gave me a new business project to do and learn every week. This just made my anxiety levels go through the roof.

Fortunately, I found a new coach who worked well for me, since needing spiritual processes along with the business ones were essential to my growth. The wrong coach was someone saying they were "spiritual" and creating nausea in me every time they said that, like my last coach. The difference was so obvious to me.

Those new business techniques really tested me. It has been very frustrating to realize I learn somewhat slower than I did when I graduated with honors from UCLA. My memory should be better! Where did you go, brain?

When I got my first computer years ago, I wouldn't touch it for two years because it frightened me. Finally, I started working on it. It has been necessary to learn to do many new things online such as classes and teleseminars. Yikes! With each new method or technique, I faced fear and discomfort. But I finally learned these newfangled techniques.

Just imagine someone like me, who was uncomfortable even touching a computer, running a telesummit! Come on, God, and all the angels from the light, be with me. Help me. Run the equipment for me. I'd pray and meditate, yet I wouldn't be consistent in my spiritual or emotional release practices. We all know being consistent works much better than being sporadic. But I did what I did. Of course, if you get scared and tighten your body out of fear, you increase your mistakes!

I simply needed all the help I could get.

Doing a telesummit was really a huge deal for me, but I did it. My program on Activate Prosperity from Heart Energy seemed to come through me and I began to come back financially. Many have been struggling with finances, not only me – how to make money, how to hold on to it, how to trust themselves to handle it in the best way possible. The big issue for many, including me, was how to make wiser decisions.

For me, the greatest awareness for moving upwards financially is the heart or *love and abundance connection*. The more deeply I'd experience love and God, the more easily abundance seemed to flow to me. Once I included learning *new business methods* and *taking action*, the pieces all really fell into place.

Recently I have created a program called "Develop Your Business Intuition." I knew I had to help people develop their intuitive abilities *and* use them for business by *listening to their guidance*. Clearly, this was another part of my biggest lesson.

By 2012 my income was up to six figures and growing.

My Big Lessons

While some coaches do inner work as well, I am really a healer and a psychotherapist. More and more I do long distance therapy and healing work, or I should really say Spirit, my guides and the healing team do the work. I just let the energy and intuition come through me.

This means I have to continually work on me to keep my energy up and clear. Since I am the vehicle, I must be open, fully present, connected to God, connected to my guides. Actually, this is what feels so fantastic for me.

When I've gone inside and asked, "So why did I have to hit rock bottom financially?" The answer that came is I was guided years ago to make products, such as recordings of what I was doing. But I was "so busy" that I didn't find time to do that. I paid the price. I didn't have online products and programs already in place when the economic crisis hit. You can be certain I am doing it now.

SO HERE ARE A COUPLE OF HUGE LESSONS I TOOK AWAY FROM THIS EXPERIENCE:

1. Remember that I am in charge. From now on, I will make sure I give personal approval before any property I own is rented to tenants. I'm very good at sensing what kinds of people are involved in different personal and business situations. I was doing that for years for clients and now it is essential that I do the same thing for myself.

2. Make sure I own a rental property I can check on regularly myself, in a location that I can easily get to.

3. Do not purchase a second or third property, unless I can undoubtedly cover all the mortgages. A basic principle, but one I just ignored.

4. The big one – **Listen to what my guides are telling me.** If it seems difficult, question it and ask for more details and guidance.

5. When our life or world seems to fall apart and we experience confusion, the death of what worked before, physical illness, emotional despair or financial ruin and desperation, we experience what is termed Shamanic Death.

6. If we follow our path, it can take us to a Rebirth, a Resurrection or a Phoenix rising out of the ashes. From that profound growth, we often experience a huge gift from Spirit that comes to us in the form of a deeper understanding of our soul's purpose.

The Gift in My Lessons

In addition to valuable lessons from these experiences, there have been numerous and incredible gifts. Now I finally recognize why it was so important for me to create classes and programs online.

For many years, I knew I had a gift of being clairsentient, or a visceral psychic, as one of the past presidents of the International Association of Past Life Therapy used to call me. I had not recognized that I'm also clairvoyant and claircognizant. This means it is easy for me to sense someone's energy body system, even by phone or during a class online. I actually get a mirror image of a person as though they are right in front of me. I'll see energy blockages and get pictures or a story that makes sense when I share it with them.

Clients began calling me from all over the United States as well as other countries to do remote healing and medical intuitive work, as well as help with prosperity issues, relationships problems and business guidance.

The more I am engaged in this type of work, the better I feel emotionally, physically, mentally and spiritually. While I am doing this type of work, what I feel is the most beautiful, profound, deeply loving energy coming from God to me and through me. I am in the perfect place. There is no other place for me to be except right here in the moment.

These kinds of experiences would never have happened if I had not listened to my guides to go online. I had no clue this was part of my path to take my work to a much bigger level. I was content before.

Like many people I work with, we need to be kicked in the butt to get out of our comfort zone to grow emotionally, mentally, physically, spiritually and energetically, and really do the work so we can live our life's purpose. If I hadn't been hurting financially, I never would have done the kinds of things I'm doing now.

The Tools That Brought Me Out of a Financial Pit

One of the most foundational tools I use is a Grounding Process. It is essential in order to be fully present. I ground frequently. If you are anxious or can get lost in your head, grounding is a necessity. It calms your energy and allows you to get quiet inside.

Someone who is not grounded can come across as *spacey, scattered, absent-minded or not in their body.* Being grounded means you feel your connection to the earth. This enables you to communicate more effectively with Spirit, intuition and your Inner Guides.

GROUNDING EXERCISE

1. Sit comfortably in a chair or lie down.
2. Slowly take in a few deep breaths and slowly let them out.
3. Imagine a warm, beautiful golden light coming in through the crown of your head.
4. Imagine that light filling you and moving down your body.
5. Feel that warm golden light move down your spine to your legs and feet.
6. Imagine energy cords or tree trunks coming out through the tailbone and the soles of your feet all the way down into the center of the Earth (called Mother Earth by Native Americans).
7. Feel your energy cords or tree trunks circling around the core of the Earth and plugging into it, securing you in the earth energy and giving you freedom.
8. Breathe that warm, moist, loving earth energy up through the Earth's crust into your feet, legs, torso, and your entire body.
9. Feel yourself connected to this powerful source of living energy. Feel its aliveness in you.

This is from my Develop Your Business Intuition Manual, Chapter 3. I actually use this as part of my Heaven and Earth Meditation.

OPENING TO SPIRIT

1. Surround yourself with a beautiful golden white light.
2. Once you've grounded and opened your body energy, take your awareness up to the top of your head.
3. Imagine Light cords or filaments coming out through the crown of your head and going up as high as you can imagine towards Spirit.
4. Breathe in that golden light from above and allow it to fully come down and move into and around your body.
5. Focus on breathing in light into your heart and breathing out any stress or tension.
6. Breathe in love energy and breathe out love on your outbreath.
7. Each time you breathe in love, let it fill a larger and larger area in your chest.
8. Breathe in love and allow it to fill your torso.
9. Breathe in love and let it fill your entire body.
10. Breathe in light and love, feeling it expand six inches (15 centimeters) around your body.

In addition to doing meditations like this a couple of times a day, I did many healing and clearing processes taken from Awakening Emotional Freedom Techniques, Hypnosis, NLP, Shamanic Healing Work and Shamanic Journeys.

Recently, my guides gave me a process to be able to more easily write articles and this chapter. This is a process to be able to listen inside and more fully hear your inner guidance.

WRITING WITH SPIRIT AND INNER GUIDANCE

1. Ground.
2. Feel Mother Earth.
3. Focus on the love, quiet, deep, slow moving energy.
4. Feel your energy align with the Earth's energy.
5. From that energy, open, clear and balance all your chakras up your body.
6. Enter your sacred heart space and the inner chamber.

7. Follow this by fully expanding and opening to Spirit.
8. Move the assemblage point of your energy system for receiving information from Spirit and Inner Guidance.
9. Thank Spirit and Inner Guidance.
10. Write as quickly as you can on your return.

This has been an interesting process for me. The first time I put all the big pieces together of what brought me back from the pits of what felt like financial death.

The Steps to Activating Prosperity with Divine Intervention

1. The first step is always come from love and from being heart-centered to really create prosperity for you in the right way.
2. Connect with Spirit and inner guidance. Listen and follow the guidance you receive. Be grateful for all the positive evidences that you are not alone.
3. Learn new business methods and techniques when necessary to take you to the next level.
4. Use emotional and spiritual processes to release any negative or lower level energies that surface along the way.
5. Take inspired action by connecting with your Higher Self.
6. If you are still having difficulties, find the right mentor, healer, psychotherapist or coach to work with you. We often have difficulty getting through those stuck places on our own.

It is my deepest desire that the story of my journey out of financial hell will assist you in your path to get to your highest level of prosperity with Divine Intervention.

Thank you! Thank you! Thank you! I gratefully thank you, Spirit, my Inner and Outer Guides, for all your assistance and guidance to help on my journey of rising out of the ashes to Soar!

I am so excited to see where the next step takes me – and you!

Love, Blessings and JOY!
Helaine

❧ ❧ ❧ ❧

HELAINE Z. HARRIS, LMFT, (United States) empowers heart-centered clients to transform their lives and businesses to reflect their authentic selves, helping people to magnetize love, power, abundance and the right clients. An intuitive business coach, shamanic healer, and psychotherapist, she is founder of An Awakening Center www.AnAwakeningCenter.com

Called the *wound detector* by her clients, with her 35 years of experience and mastery of energy, Helaine has helped thousands of clients awaken their potential and manifest it in their daily lives. She is the author of the award-winning book, *Are You in Love with a Vampire? Healing the Relationship Drain Game.* www.hzharris.com

 HELAINE'S FREE GIFT: Meet Your Prosperity Guide Package, including private Prosperity Breakthrough Session with Helaine at HTTP://EMBRACEDBYTHEDIVINE.COM/GET-YOUR-BONUS-GIFTS/

How I Lost My Money and Found My Spirit

– Therese Skelly

Never in a million years did I think I'd be sitting in that horrible place known as bankruptcy court. How in the world did a well-educated, smart, driven woman end up losing her house, car, credit score, and self-respect? What happened that led me to have that very dark night of the soul where my life as I knew it was rapidly slipping through my fingertips?

Today I see it as Divine Intervention. But for the long, horribly painful time when I was wrestling with trying to keep my financial life in order, I sure didn't see God in the mix.

Nope. Fear, terror, anxiety, and shame were my constant companions. What I didn't know then was that that experience of losing everything would not only bring me to my knees, it would finally be the very thing that allowed me to step into a deepening of my experience of the knowing that "God's gotcha." I came out on the other side having really lived into a sense of faith and trust that today allows me to have a glorious life and profitable business.

So let me share the story and what I learned so you can (hopefully) not suffer like I did.

I was "Cinderella," except I didn't know that at the time. Here I was; a talented woman married to a man who made very good money. I felt like a feminist in that I believed in my strength, made all the decisions in the household, had a Master's degree, didn't feel like I needed a man, and thought I was very self-reliant.

Then one day after 18 years, my then-husband decided he was unhappy and wanted to leave. There is no pain greater than having to tell your children that their parents are separating. My boys, ages six and 10 at the time, were devastated. I was angry, numb, and had no idea how I'd be able to be a single parent or make enough money to support me and the boys.

Initially I left with a large chunk of alimony. I had two big clients, so my income was over $10,000 a month from those three sources. But then the recession hit. The ex was no longer able to pay me what he was supposed to, the marketing client left, and the other contract I had also decided to terminate our agreement. So I went from a wonderful monthly income to making less than $2,000 a month. Actually, in my lowest month I brought in only $700, which wouldn't even cover food for the boys. In the meantime, I'd bought a sports car, blown through all my savings, and was watching my money, my sanity, and everything else slip away.

This is where the battle began.

See, I never had the father figure that I could lean on. He was around, but we weren't close, and any message I got from him was usually related to what was wrong with me. Today I see that he was very troubled, and emotionally unavailable. With my past training as a therapist, I know that very often women who have strained relationships with their dads have a tremendously difficult time believing in a God who will support them.

If you have never been loved unconditionally, nor had someone there to protect you, the belief that you will be taken care of by a Higher Power is just not something you have access to. All the faith in the world cannot fill the wound of an absent father, so a woman has a difficult time with the concept of surrender and trust.

And sadly, during the very time when I most needed to lean on something like God to know that I'd be okay, I struggled with it the greatest. Having grown up not being able to rely on my father for love and emotional support, I learned that I had to create my life and make it what I wanted. Sure I went to church. I absolutely had a connection with the Divine. I was no stranger to spiritual seeking. But it was not enough to allow me to trust and surrender to what was happening.

During this scary and intense time, the fight for me then became not the fight of good/evil, but rather strong/weak....Faith versus fear.

In reality it became the entrepreneur part versus the scared little girl part. Every night I would lie awake in my bed feeling just terrified. Nothing I did could ever soothe my constant level of anxiety. I had visions of losing my house, having to get rid of my dog, and sleeping on the floor of my ex's two-bedroom apartment. (Because of our kids, he would not ever let me be homeless, but was not in the financial position to do anything to help. And giving up my dog was certainly not a viable option.)

The little girl in me wanted to be rescued. She wanted someone to help, save, or fix her. She doubted her ability and just wanted to crumble and collapse. But then the more powerful entrepreneurial part in me would come to the table saying, "I cannot give up." Frankly, I fancied myself pretty unemployable because I'd let my professional therapy license go, and I had no interest in working a job for someone else. So the only option I would ever allow myself would be to see how I could turn my business around and make it profitable.

But I could not do this alone. Each night I'd do my best managing the battles in my head. At times the anxiety was debilitating. I'd barely sleep and my health was jeopardized. The stress was getting the best of me in that I was having heart palpitations, gaining weight, and frankly, I am amazed that I didn't have a breakdown during this period.

What saved me? My girlfriends began to take a stand for me. My friend Molly had coaching sessions with me once or twice a week. She called on her "Divine Team" and did clearing and EFT (Emotional Freedom Technique) to help me calm my jagged nervous system.

Another friend, Mitzi, who is a Religious Science Minister, used to have daily calls where she'd pray with me, helping me know the Truth that God was also in this situation and that the resolution was already handled. Her wise counsel was finally the thing that helped me get a handle on my emotions. Mitzi would gently say, "Therese, even though you don't SEE the outcome changing right now, can you GIVE THANKS ahead of time?

Can you know with me that God has already handled everything for you? Everything you need is already on its way. Can you take a moment and say a little prayer of gratitude?"

This became the turning point. Between Mitzi's loving words, and reading Pastor Joel Osteen's book, *It's Your Time*, I slowly became able to have little minutes of peace. In the beginning, I'd slip right back into fear and anxiety, but now I had tools. I'd remember Rev. Mitzi's words or pick up Joel's book and be reminded that God had EVERYTHING handled. I started to take the steps necessary to release my house, sports car, and debt.

Was it painful and shameful? Oh, heck yeah! I wasn't raised to be one of those gals who walked away from responsibility. Yet this was the right choice for me. I did what I had to do to clean up my financial situation and was determined never to make those mistakes again.

In fact, one of my favorite stories from this time happened on the day of the bankruptcy hearing. When I went to court, it ended up being on a day where I had planned on flying to Las Vegas to attend a business event. So I went to the hearing and got a ride from the court to the airport. The first night of the event I was at the VIP party. One of my peers (who is today a multi-millionaire coach) came up to me and said, "Therese, I see you everywhere and hear such wonderful things about you. You are doing GREAT, aren't you?"

In this moment I could have shared the shameful story of JUST being in bankruptcy court a few hours earlier. But I saw in that moment that God had sent me an angel to let me know that while the *material stuff* of my life had fallen away, who I was becoming and the journey I was on made me GREAT. I immediately got the message, so smiled sweetly and said to her, "Yeah, I AM doing really well today." A huge lesson in what matters and an even bigger triumph in that I allowed the message in from Spirit that, indeed, all was well.

Let me tell you how I turned the corner.

Basically, I stopped being a drama queen!

That sounds funny, but because of having a painful childhood, challenging marriage, divorce, and financial wreckage, let's just say I had lots of stories about how things were hard for me.

I hired a coach and paid her $20,000 to help me shift my mindset. What I noticed is that when she asked me what I wanted, I'd tell her all the back story of how things never worked, how it had been so hard, etc.

I realized that I had so many traumas in my energy that I was constantly recycling that pain.

Knowing what we know about how important it is to be in vibrational alignment with our desire, it makes sense that for a time after my bankruptcy was discharged, I still struggled. You see, I hadn't made the shift in the area of my BEING to be able to be different.

What was missing is that I had to come to peace with what had happened. Even though the bankruptcy was behind me, when I tried to set goals, I felt blocked because I felt like I had to hide a huge part of my life. The exercise of visioning my bright future and making plans for the six-figure business I desired got derailed because, unbeknownst to me, I was still struggling with shame. Here I was, a business coach, helping people make more money and yet I'd messed up my life by mismanaging mine.

The little voice inside kept asking me why people should trust me and challenged my credibility because of my past mistakes. Let me just say that it's quite hard to market and sell yourself when you have this stuff pulling at you in the background!

But again, God is good and always provides the right solution at the right time. At my coach's retreat we were setting up our ideal futures. Here I got hit with the awareness that there was no way in the world I could live into my goals because of the secret I was carrying. I burst into tears and shared this with the women in the room. And the most amazing thing happened.

One of my peers looked at me lovingly and said, "Therese, actually I'd be MORE likely to hire you now because of what you shared about your bankruptcy and what you've learned from it. I'd feel like you could understand me and would be compassionate as a coach as well."

Yet again Spirit calmed those voices by sending someone who at the right time gave me the perfect message to move forward.

It was then and there that I decided to tell the story. Not just tell the story, but make it my life's work to help women overcome their money challenges and tap into their God-given gifts to create businesses they would love. And you know what happens when you make a declaration, right?

Two days after the retreat, while listening in meditation, I got the message from Sprit that I was to do a telesummit called "Breaking Down to Break Free." No playing small for me! Nope. This story wasn't going to be told to just a few people. My big reveal was going to be out and in a very public way. I hosted an amazing line-up of speakers who all shared their breakdown stories.

My goal was that no woman should ever feel shame again, so by bringing top experts who shared their journeys, I was able to accomplish just that. Hundreds of people heard stories of loss, surrender, and then how to strengthen their faith and turn their lives and business around. Doing this made me realize the huge blessing that my bankruptcy was. It showed me that if I can own it and transform it, I can then teach this to my wonderful clients.

But I had just a bit more work to do before it finally happened.

That drama queen in me was settling down a bit, but I still had the sense that money was "out there" somewhere. I began doing okay in my business, but the shift for me came when I finally learned to align and understand that money is here now. I completely reframed my relationship with God and Money. I viewed money as energy and love and instead of looking at the lack, I created an absolute conviction that because I was in alignment with my purpose/passion, I should and could be rewarded for it.

And this is where my very powerful teaching was birthed.

I came to realize there is what I call *the meantime*. That means that you do the work and plant the seed that you wish to see come to fruition. But very often, this takes time. It's in this time that faith is the necessary ingredient.

Here's how I explain it to my clients: Think about the farmer. He doesn't go in every day pulling the seed up, checking to see if it's still there. Actually, what happens is that LIFE provides all that the seed needs. The seed actually is equipped to draw to itself all the nutrients it needs to begin to sprout. The very act of putting the seed in the ground activates the knowing of the innate wisdom of how to fulfill its purpose and destiny.

This is the ultimate example of faith, isn't it? We get an intuitive hit about what we'd like to do or have or be, and then take action. We never know where it's going to end up, but the faith is what allows us to be true to that dream in spite of sometimes not seeing any tangible progress.

This process is how I've created a multi six-figure business. Even in spite of the "evidence" that I wasn't reaching my goals, I have learned to be in constant faith that I am always supported and provided for. This means that I take inspired action, do what I'm called to do, then *rest in God*, knowing that it's all being handled.

It's been the most amazing journey. The gift of hitting bottom and then being able to spring back so powerfully is what makes me the woman I am today. If I were to give you a list of what to do if you are facing challenges, it would be this:

1. Admit you need help.
2. Reach out and allow people you trust to take care of you when you need.
3. Examine your relationship with God/Spirit/Source and determine how able you are to surrender to that and know that you are being supported all the time.
4. Find books or inspirational material that will keep you grounded when you need to be reminded of your faith.
5. Focus on what you want rather than on what you don't.

6. Be willing to invest whatever you need to for your personal development.
7. Dream big and know that the real work is you releasing anything that will interfere with getting that dream out in the world.
8. Adopt a never-give-up attitude.
9. Let your pain or your "mess" become your message. Don't be afraid to share it because, more than likely, you can be an inspiration to others.
10. Always focus on gratitude and good in your life. Even the most painful lessons are of Divine Design.

Money mindset mentor and business coach THERESE SKELLY (United States) works with heart-centered entrepreneurs who love what they do and are ready to grow their business in a much easier and more authentic way. Blending her background as a psychotherapist, strategist, and business consultant, she masterfully works both the inner game challenges and the outer game tactics. From newer business owners to already successful entrepreneurs, Therese works with individuals who desire to make a big difference in the world. Get her free five-part video series Eliminating Money Blocks by visiting www.HAPPYINBUSINESS.COM

 THERESE'S FREE GIFT: Mindset Mastery eBook at HTTP:// EMBRACEDBYTHEDIVINE.COM/GET-YOUR-BONUS-GIFTS/

Back to Health
– Joanne Newell

"You look like Quasimodo," smirked my sister as I virtually dragged my right leg behind me up the driveway.

I grimaced at her, fully aware of how awful I looked. I hoped the neighbors weren't able to see me as I lurched along.

We had just waved off family who'd come to visit, and my sister was about to head off, too. My husband, Darren, helped me up the two steps into our house, and I hobbled slowly to our bedroom so that I could lie down on my left side and let my right leg's burning pain and cramping ease just a little.

My back problem had become a *very bad* back problem.

I was in excruciating pain, even though I was taking anti-inflammatories and strong painkillers.

It was September of 2007, and my little twin daughters were soon to turn five years of age. I couldn't believe that I was only 36, yet I was walking about like a hunched-over 100-year-old lady.

It had all started when I was 12 years old – on the first day in my "advanced" figure roller-skating class, I had fallen down hard onto my bottom and had hurt my back. The specialist said I had sprained a ligament.

From that time on, I seemed to have more and more troubles with my back ... perhaps from carrying a large, heavy, schoolbag on one shoulder for too many years, perhaps from sedentary office jobs (and, if I'm honest, perhaps too sedentary a lifestyle), and perhaps from having a twin pregnancy and lifting toddlers, a disc in my lower back said, "No more!" and proceeded to rudely push its sticky innards against the nerves nestled next to it.

This sent shooting pains down my right leg, and stiffened my lower back.

I'd always been intensely interested in personal development, and I had an inkling that this "back" issue had more meaning than just its physical reality.

I had been reading Louise Hay's *You Can Heal Your Life*, and recognized that problems with the lower back represent a feeling that the Universe is not supporting you – that you don't trust that you'll be supported monetarily.

I definitely resonated with that, with me being a stay-at-home mum and working part-time as a freelance book editor (let's just say that many editors live in "genteel poverty" for the sake of doing work that they love).

I'd always been fearful of money – although I always wanted more of it, I didn't really believe that I would ever have enough to do all that I wanted.

There was another gift of realization in all of this, too. At the time, I was a subscriber to a life coach named Vicky White. A few months before my back became really bad, Vicky had sent out an email sharing information about a raw-food cleanse program being run by a new business called The Raw Divas.

I had dabbled with raw food in my mid-teens, but hadn't been able to keep up that way of life while still living at home – even though I purchased my own blender and food processor (for making yummy salads, dressings and fruit-and-nut treats from Leslie Kenton's *Raw Energy* recipe book) when I started my first part-time job. I had attempted to do raw cleanses at various times in my 20s, but never really stuck to them.

So I found it really interesting that raw food made another appearance in my life, especially when I was facing a health crisis.

I realized that I hadn't been paying enough attention to my health. My priority had been looking after my two little girls, and fitting in freelance work on weekends, all fueled by coffee and a lot of chocolate (I'm sure many of you can relate to that!).

I decided to take the plunge and invest in the raw-food cleanse, which was a 30-day group program that included menu planners, shopping lists, fitness tips and other fantastic coaching materials. There were supportive group calls, and a forum. I was thrilled to have found a community of women around the world who were also on a quest for better health, and I was so pleased that Tera and Amy (the owners of The Raw Divas at the time) had put together such a fantastic program.

By that time, we no longer had a blender, so I borrowed my aunt's blender and started whipping up fruit smoothies from the program's recipe selection. They were unbelievably good! I then bravely tried a few green smoothies, starting slowly at first by adding just a few green leaves to fruit smoothies. I also started giving these fruit and green smoothies to my girls.

At some stage, as my back problem became worse, I wondered if eating a largely raw diet would actually help to heal my back. At the very least, it would help me lose a little bit of weight (not that I was overweight), which may have been helpful if I ended up needing – gulp – surgery.

So, we decided to buy our own blender, which, with heavy everyday use, including making nut milks, didn't last long. A strange burning smell from the motor soon let us know that we were working it too hard. Because I knew that smoothies were going be a big part of my life, I took a deep breath and invested in a state-of-the-art Vitamix blender. Oh my goodness, what a difference ... silky-smooth smoothies whipped up in no time at all!

It felt a little strange to be taking seemingly "extreme" measures with my health, by eating high raw, while at the same time gulping down painkillers and anti-inflammatories. What a contradiction! But there wasn't any way that I could function without those tablets, at the time.

I remember once laying on my left side on our bed, doing some writing work (which I'll explain more about in just a second...), when I lost track of time and realized that I'd forgotten to take my tablets. My little girls had been playing quietly on the floor in my room, and when I tried to get up, I knew that I'd waited too long.

I could not move. Literally.

Luckily, my girls were old enough to be able to help. I asked them to take a little chair into the office, and to step on the chair to reach the phone. They could then bring the phone to me so that I could call my grandmother, who lived a few minutes away and could come and get my tablets from the high shelf in the kitchen cupboard.

I remember thinking at the time: "This is ridiculous. I can't even look after my children properly because of my stupid back. What if they fall over and hurt themselves and I can't help them?"

It was around this time that I also had to stop driving. My right leg was so weak from nerve damage that there was no way I could safely drive.

I had to humble myself by accepting help from other mothers at my girls' kindergarten, who would kindly collect the girls after kindergarten sessions and take them to their homes to play with their children. Darren would then collect them after work.

I felt like a "bad mother," and, after a lifetime of being a "can do," independent person, it didn't feel good to have to accept help and to rely on others. I knew, though, as with the trust and health lessons I was learning, this was another lesson that was revealing itself. It really is OK to accept help. You don't have to be perfect, and you don't have to "do it all."

A few months before things had become that bad, and at around the same time as I rediscovered raw foods (Coincidence? Of course not!), I was asked by a local publisher to modernize and revamp an old, out-of-print recipe book for children. The publishers wanted the new title to be *I'm Hungry, Let's Cook!*

Having edited food books at Lonely Planet before my girls were born, I was passionate about scrumptious food and recipes – and with my renewed passion for health, I knew that I needed to get a message of health into this book. Having children also gave me a great perspective on what children wanted and were capable of doing in the kitchen.

I jumped at the chance, and I ended up completely rewriting the book.

I used a few of the original recipes but expanded their explanations to help novice chefs, and I ended up creating most of the book's recipes from scratch. Having experienced some badly written recipes in my time, I was keen to test each recipe three times.

However, the testing phase came at a very painful stage in my back's decline.

I remember leaning heavily on my left forearm, against the kitchen bench, to take the weight off of my back and my right leg, and then struggling to stir together ingredients and rewrite measurements and instructions on my recipe-in-progress printouts. It's kind of a pathetic picture, when you think about it, although I kept muddling through, determined to create a high-quality book, to deadline.

I also remember feeling torn – with my personal, newfound passion for uncooked, healthy foods, I didn't want to include any "unhealthy" recipes at all in this book for children. Even having the word "cook" in the book's title felt like a betrayal of my commitment to healthy eating, which, for me, meant mainly raw foods.

However, the publisher really wanted the book to include recipes that appealed to a mainstream market.

How could I reconcile my beliefs with the requests of the publisher?

I eventually realized that, by including "less-healthy" recipe options, such as for cupcakes, in the book, it would appeal to mainstream parents – but I could sneakily weave in health messages. I added features on using fresh, home-grown produce, and I promoted the use of organic, high-quality products. The book would be a bridge from the mainstream to a healthier way of eating! Raw-food recipes such as Raspberry and Banana Smoothie and Banana-Blueberry Creamy Freeze sat alongside recipes for French toast and cookies.

(As it happened, the same publisher later asked me to write an organic gardening and recipe book for children – called *I'm Hungry, Let's Grow It!* – and this gave me the chance to include a green smoothie recipe and to go even further with promoting organic and healthy eating.)

At least I had this new project to take my attention off of the worsening state of my back. It was also good to know that I'd be making income from the book (thank you, Universe!).

When my herniated-disc back symptoms first started to become serious, my gorgeous, kind physiotherapist valiantly suggested a course of intensive treatment, regularly manipulating and massaging the area. She also suggested that I purchase a portable TENS machine, which did help to relax the muscles between treatments.

I'm a pretty optimistic person at heart, so I fully expected that a bit of massage and TLC would do the trick. I'd had back flare-ups before and I'd always "come good," so this would all work out. Wouldn't it?

However, when it became apparent that physiotherapy treatment wasn't going to work (and my higher consumption of raw foods wasn't going to be enough to heal my body at that point), I agreed to try having a cortisone injection at a local hospital. Much to the dismay of the anesthetist, the treatment made my pain worse, as it seemed to have moved things around to create a fresh area of pain. At times I could barely breathe – the pain was so raw. Getting in and out of the passenger seat of a car took minutes and was an awkward, excruciating process.

I was starting to become frightened, but I also had a deeper sense that I would be OK, no matter what. I felt that the Universe was looking out for me, and that whatever pain I was going through now would only be temporary – good would come. But it was still frustrating...

When I look back now, I feel sad that, on a couple of brief occasions, I let myself fall deep into self-pity, and to wonder whether I would ever walk properly again, if at all.

It became clear that I needed surgery. I could no longer feel the big toe on my right leg, and to leave it any longer could possibly have meant permanent nerve damage.

I had already booked in for January to see a surgeon reputed to be "The Best," according to my nurse-friend, but by October the pain was getting beyond ridiculous.

The surgeon agreed to see me early, and when he saw my MRI results and the pain I was in, he booked me in for immediate surgery, in two days' time. Fortunately, we had invested in private hospital cover a few years before having children.

I really couldn't believe that I would be having surgery. What about the risks? I tried to stop myself thinking about the fact that people DIE in surgery. How could I bear to think about leaving my two little girls behind, without a mum?

How on earth had it come to this?

The morning of the day I was due to go to hospital, I finalized my recipe-book manuscript and gave it to Darren to put in the post. I remember thinking (rather dramatically, I guess), "Well, if I die, then at least I have the legacy of this book and the girls can be proud of me!"

My beautiful girls clambered gently onto the bed and kissed me goodbye before Darren helped walk me out to the car.

Knowing that I was going into a potentially dangerous situation, life was put into sharp contrast. I realized just how much I appreciated the life that I had, and that I was being given a huge gift in the entire experience.

I also knew that I was in the best hands possible for surgery.

But even knowing that, it didn't stop me from crying as I lay in my softly lit hospital room on the night before the operation. I pulled out a notebook that I'd brought with me. Laying heavily on my left side, I wrote each of my daughters a long note from the heart, letting them know how much I loved them, how proud I was of them, some special memories that I had of them, and of my hopes for their future. I also let them know that if anything happened to me, I would always be there, watching over them. I wrote until my hand ached.

I also asked the Universe to look after me. To have the surgery be a success. To let me come through, alive and healed, so that I could continue to be mother to my girls. I also promised that, if I came through it, I would use my life to help others, and to do the work I was meant to do.

The last thing I remember is lying on my hospital bed, looking up and watching thin fluorescent lights pass above me as I was wheeled down the hospital aisle by two orderlies.

The surgery was a success. Almost straight away I could feel that my right leg had been relieved of nerve pressure. I still couldn't feel my big toe (and it's still slightly numb, even to this day), but I was happy to be alive and to know that I would soon be able to walk again!

I was driven home by ambulance. I wasn't allowed to sit for six weeks after the surgery, so an ambulance was the only way to get me home safely in a laying-down position.

I arrived home on a beautifully sunny spring day. My bed was gently wheeled out of the vehicle, and the two cheery ambulance workers carefully helped me to stand up. I remember noticing how lovely the leaves on our front-garden tree looked. How the sun sparkled on them. Everything seemed so alive, and I could feel the warm air caressing my skin.

My girls had, by this time, raced out of the house and were watching me with wide eyes and big smiles. "Mummy, Mummy! Come inside and look what we've done for you!"

They grabbed my hands and tried to urge me along the driveway but were then reminded that I had to go slowly, so they eased up their speed.

Darren helped me up the steps, and when I turned into our living room, I saw a beautiful handmade banner pinned up on the back wall. It said, "Welcome Home Mummy!"

Our bed was also in the living room where the lounge suite had been. Darren had moved it out into our open-plan living area so that I could be part of family life during my recovery, rather than lying on my own in the bedroom.

My heart felt like it was overflowing. I saw the blessing in the situation for Darren and the girls, in that they got to experience the profound pleasure of giving, and of being so very thoughtful, loving and considerate.

I was so grateful to be home with my family, and to know that the surgery had been a success. I was on the road to recovery.

I've kept my promise to the Universe and have let it work through me. I've been able to be here, fully, for my girls, and I went on to write that second book (*I'm Hungry, Let's Grow It!*), and a third book called *Monkey Mike's Raw Food Kitchen: An Un-Cookbook for Kids!* (the world's first raw-food recipe e-book for children – you can see Mike at www.monkeymikeskitchen.com).

I also went on to create a life-coaching business called Rich Radiant Real, which was a Law-of-Attraction-based business that helped women with wealth, health and happiness – and I've now evolved further, helping enlightened entrepreneurial women create an empowered money mindset, in my new business called Rich Life by Design.

These amazing businesses came about because of my continued willingness to listen to the messages of Spirit. That painful period of life offered a huge wake-up call. I faced my mortality and was woken up to trusting the Universe to support me. I really "got" the importance of looking after my body-temple... And that it's OK to accept help from others.

Everything really does happen for a reason, and even if life isn't always perfect, I know that, if I continue to be conscious and aware, everything works out for my highest good.

I know my life is being used in a powerful way, and I am so grateful and honored to be able to do that. I really am blessed, and I hope my story helps others see that the painful events of their lives have a profound purpose and can be a catalyst for deeper growth.

I must say, though – I'm very grateful that I no longer look like Quasimodo!

JOANNE NEWELL (Australia) knows, to the depths of her soul, that enlightened, spirit-driven entrepreneurial women are here to change the world. They're here to live a full, rich life, and to help others and the planet. She also knows that money makes it possible for them to do all of this, so she helps women create an empowered money mindset. She reveals how to create a rich life, by design (in co-creation with Spirit). If you'd like to start creating a money mindset that works for you then visit HTTP://WWW.RICHLIFEBYDESIGN.COM

JOANNE'S FREE GIFT: The 3 Foundations of an Empowered Money Mindset – 3-part video series at HTTP://EMBRACEDBYTHEDIVINE.COM /GET-YOUR-BONUS-GIFTS/

The Gift of Adversity
– Kerri Kannan

The Setup

On December 28, 2011, on my 41st birthday, I found myself alone in my small apartment, feeling desperate and looking for answers. My kids were with their dad for the Christmas holiday, and I had gotten myself into a financial situation from which I did not know how I would recover.

Three years before, my ex-husband and I had gone through a very thorough mediation process and had a somewhat amicable divorce. There was no indication then that finalizing our divorce would not be the end of the problems experienced during our marriage, but was really only the beginning. I had no idea that my ex-husband and I would be going through multiple custody battles. I had decided to end the marriage because I no longer wanted to expose myself and my children to the emotional roller-coaster, but the end of the marriage was only the beginning of the nightmare.

Looking back, I can see where every challenge has had a silver lining and the more difficult the challenge, the more valuable the hidden gifts have been disguised within those challenges. My challenges with my ex-husband and the financial difficulties I had as a result are no exception.

My relationship with my ex-husband has been the most difficult of my life and at times, even though it is very easy to blame him for my hardships, he is also the one who has pushed me relentlessly to reclaim my power in ways I never imagined I could. In that, he has been one of my greatest gifts. It is, however, not always easy to remember that gift.

Very early in our marriage, he suggested that I quit my job and figure out what I really wanted to do. That "permission slip" allowed me to set out on a search for my life purpose, which I discuss in great detail in my book, *Uncovering the Divine Within – A Journey of Self-Love*. I realized that my life purpose was the exact opposite of what I perceived to be my flaws, challenges and disowned aspects of self. It was up to me to heal the disconnect within my mind, learn to love, trust and believe in myself and to teach others how to do the same. I believe we all have a similar purpose: to heal the fragmented aspects of ourselves and learn to love and accept ourselves fully. Only then can we be non-judgmental and forgiving toward ourselves and others as we allow our true divine nature to shine through, unfiltered.

I also believe we are never given more than we can take at any given moment, although I do wish sometimes that the Universe did not have so much faith in my ability to overcome adversity!

That birthday-evening, on December 28, 2011, I knew I needed a change. During the two years prior, my ex-husband and I had engaged in four court battles, including two custody battles and two modification of support hearings. These left me financially devastated, living in a small apartment, bankrupt, and my well-constructed, mediated custody agreement looked nothing like it did when we created it four years earlier. My custody share was reduced from my having primary custody, every weekday and every third weekend, to having joint shared custody with a 50/50 split and there was always a looming threat of another full-blown custody battle.

I realized that this mess was created, not by accident but because I had given too much of my power away in order to maintain peace within the relationship. The very thing I felt was being used to control me, my love for my kids, was the exact thing that would be the driving force behind the reclaiming of my power and freeing myself from the cycle.

Through the months that preceded that December night, I had been receiving little intuitive nudges to get clear about what I really wanted. The holiday season in the U.S. starts in late November, so I had been putting this soul-searching off through the holidays, but since I didn't have my kids that particular night, my home was clean and free of distractions, I decided to take some time to figure out what I really wanted. I had no idea that making that one little decision to pay attention to that nudge would have such a profound and far reaching effect on my life.

I sat down in my little apartment and thought about what I wanted. I knew I needed a mentor to show me how to transform my financial mindset but couldn't afford to pay for one. I had worked online with a great wealth mentor, but I needed someone up-close and personal who was willing to spend time with me.

The Process

After a bit of contemplation, I decided that I wanted to have a man in my life to be my mentor, because I respond differently to men than women. I wanted someone who would help me to overcome my poverty mindset once and for all and teach me how to master the money thing. I did not want to enter a relationship with an expectation of receiving financial security in return for sexual commitment. That was what I felt got me into trouble in the first place. Sure I believed I loved my ex-husband when I got married, however, now I wonder how much of that "love" was tied up in attachments and expectations. I did not want to repeat that mistake again and wanted to get through the money thing before joining anyone in another committed relationship.

I decided that I wanted a man who was my best friend, but I wanted to keep the sexual aspect out of it, either entirely or at least until I felt strong enough within my own financial security that I could connect sexually and romantically from a place of wholeness, not need. I didn't care if my male mentor and best friend was married or gay, I just wanted there to be a barrier that would keep us from entering a sexual relationship and I wanted a best friend who would love me enough to help me figure out the financial thing without strings attached.

I knew that only love was powerful enough to pull me through my stupor so we had to have a really strong connection. I wanted our mutual adoration to be the glue that bound us, as well as the driving force behind my growth and expansion. I also wanted to be of equal service to him in his growth and expansion. I was happy to not know how I would be of service to him, I just knew that I wanted to be as much of a blessing to him

222 | Embraced by the Divine

in his life as he would be to me, and I wanted for each of us to recognize the tremendous gifts we were to each other.

From all the teachings I learned over the years, I knew that there HAD to be a way that I could create exactly what I wanted in my life but I also knew that this "system" had eluded me my entire life. I knew that after 20 years of following my own personal development path and helping others to let go of their limitations, I had to have all of the tools I needed to consciously create anything, I just didn't know how to put the pieces together and in what order.

So, I meditated on allowing the process to be revealed to me where I could be intuitively guided through each step as it happened. I didn't know what would come next; I just took one step at a time. When I felt as if one step had been completed, I asked for the next step and each step revealed itself through the process.

The following steps reveal the exact process that summoned a person in my life who EXACTLY matched the request that was put forth. Keep in mind, when the request was put out into the Universe, I didn't even know if this person existed, so I was putting something out there that was completely outside of my conscious awareness of how it could possibly happen. The process came to me intuitively so if you try this on your own, I would suggest you follow it loosely and if you intuitively feel guided to follow a slightly different course, I encourage you to trust your divine guidance. Here is how it unfolded for me:

STEP 1 – GET CLEAR

I sat down to get clear and started thinking about all the things that I wanted in a mentor. During the months prior, while getting the little nudges to get clear, the thought kept entering my mind that I wanted a romantic partner, but I had resistance to that idea because I didn't want my financial well-being to be tied to a relationship. I learned through the years to just be clear about the desire and allow the Universe to take care of the details. So my ideas settled on the possibility of a close friendship.

When I let go of thinking that I had to enter a romantic partnership, I felt my energy immediately align with the idea of having a new best friend.

This idea excited me. When I was in high school, I always had very close male friends, but as an adult, and especially after I got married, I found that it was just not possible for me to maintain male friendships. I wanted male friends, but it seemed that it was not in harmony with the dynamic of my marriage.

STEP 2 – LET GO OF RESISTANCE

Even though I was pretty clear about what I wanted, I still had some relics of past programming to deal with which kept me from completely buying into the possibility of this mystery person showing up. I knew I had to release the remaining thoughts that stood in the way of being in complete alignment with the idea. So, using Emotional Freedom Technique (EFT), I looked at each resistant thought and, one by one, I tapped through each restrictive thought or nuance until I felt completely clear of any ideas that told me I could not have this person show up in my life.

STEP 3 – ASK IN THE LANGUAGE THAT THE UNIVERSE UNDERSTANDS

This step could possibly be broken down into four action steps, but when I did it, it all felt like one step. Therefore, I have chosen to break it down in the four actions so that this part of the process is as clear to you as possible, as well as describe how I employed them in the creation process.

a) In order to manifest something, the thoughts had to get out of my head and into my heart.

b) I knew I needed to FEEL it in my body from a perspective as if the event had already happened.

c) The spoken word carries a specific physical vibration and has within it a tremendous power to create, so that had to be part of the process.

d) I walked around my apartment while performing the actions above so that I could feel in my body, what it felt like to experience the state of being I was telling the Universe I desired.

In this step, I was guided to take all four action steps above and incorporate them into one action. I already knew what I wanted and I had released my resistance to the idea, so now it was time to ask for what I wanted in a language the Universe understands. All four of the components to this Step 3 are ways of communicating with the Universe. I was simply intuitively guided to use all four at once.

I had to get my thoughts out of my head and into my heart so I simply placed my hand on my heart and spoke affirmations that the circumstances had already lined up from a perspective that it had already happened. I then walked around my apartment and spoke out loud the things that I wanted to feel as a result of this connection. I said things like, "I love that I have this new best friend, who is helping me, once and for all, to really learn how to claim my power as it relates to money. I love that I am as much of a gift to him and all I need to do is just be me. I love that we feel such a great connection and we both pull each other to grow. I love that we feel so comfortable in each other's presence that we can be completely authentic without fear of losing the friendship. I love that even though we are strongly connected, there are circumstances in the way of our forming a romantic relationship."

I walked around my apartment for several minutes, simply repeating these types of affirmations until the step just naturally morphed into Step 4.

STEP 4 – GRATITUDE

After Step 3, and all of the physical action I took, my heart felt so full of love for this idea and this creation that my narrative naturally turned into one of gratitude. Instead of walking through my apartment and repeating what I loved so much about this creation, I naturally moved into gratitude. I started saying things like, "I am so grateful that this person has shown up in my life. I am so grateful for this new best friend. I am so grateful that I am as much of a gift to him as he is me." Then it turned into a simple statement of, "Thank you, I love you. Thank you, I love you. Thank you, I love you."

It was starting to get late and I had to wake up really early the next morning to go to work, but I was so excited and energized from the idea that sleep was not going to happen. I could feel the idea buzzing with excitement throughout my entire body. At that point, I knew I had to let the idea go.

STEP 5 – LET IT GO

I knew that I had to get sleep and I also knew that I had to let the idea go out into the Universe so that the Universe could do its work. We tend to cling to the ideas of the things we want, but if we hold on to our dreams, we are keeping the Universe from doing its job. It is our job to know what we want and the Universe's job to deliver the goods.

So once again, I used EFT to let go of the idea so I could get some sleep. This time, as I tapped, the affirmations I used were more along the lines of, "Even though I love this idea, I release and let it go. Even though I am afraid to let it go because I don't know if this will ever come back to me, I am willing to trust the Universe to do its job and I release and let it go. Even though I have no idea if this is even possible, I deeply and completely accept myself and I release and let it go."

After about 20 minutes, I felt clear and relaxed enough to go to bed and sleep a very restful night.

The Manifestation

The next day, I went to see a friend who had been helping me to get a part-time home-based business off the ground that was bringing her, and many others, an annual residual income of nearly $30,000. I got into the business because I saw the potential, but soon realized that I did not have the right mindset to earn that kind of money.

She asked me something about the business and something within me told me to say, "Nancy, I appreciate all that you are doing for me but I need to work with someone who will benefit financially from my success." She said, "Okay, I am going to put you in touch with our Executive Consultant, Craig." I had never seen nor heard of this guy before and didn't even know he existed.

Nancy tried to connect us via text, but I didn't hear back at first. I called him a few days after that and I didn't know it at the time, but he had been in bed for about four months, trying to recuperate from an illness. About two years before, he had had a heart attack and open-heart surgery and his immune system was shot. I don't know if he was in bed recuperating or getting ready to give up. When I called, he heard my voice and told me to hold on a minute. He had to adjust himself and he sat up in bed, which I later found out he had not done in months. We talked for a while and seemed to really hit it off. As we became acquainted with each other, we discovered that we had very similar paths and that we both shared a birthday, December 28, only he was five years older than me.

About six weeks after I first called him, he came to New York for a conference and we decided to ride together so we could talk while we were on our drive. After we drove back from the conference, we grabbed a bite to eat and neither of us wanted to go home, so he invited me to watch him sing karaoke. We had a great time and felt like we had known each other forever. I asked him if he would just let me trail him while he goes out and trains people in the business so that I could become accustomed to his energy around money and learn more about how to work the business, as well as develop the kind of mindset that he had. He had earned over $1,000,000 in every business he had ever been involved with and I wanted some of that good mojo to rub off on me.

Something I didn't know about people who have had open-heart surgery is that panic attacks are a common result of the surgery. Craig says that the body goes through so much trauma during surgery, by being so violently ripped open, that it is hard for the psyche to recover. What I didn't realize was that often, while he is driving, he would have a panic attack while all alone on the road and sometimes they would last for over an hour. That is a long time for anyone to be in that kind of state. The first time this happened when I was in the car with him, he pulled over and told me he was having a panic attack. Being a Reiki Master, I just did what I would do naturally, which was to place a hand on each side of his chest and just let the Reiki do its work. The first time this happened, the panic attack only lasted about 20 minutes. As we spent more time together, I repeated the Reiki every time he had a panic attack and, gradually, they reduced to only three minutes by the time he left New York and went back to Texas.

It took me probably two to three months to realize that on December 28, when I asked for this person to show up, that it was put into motion almost immediately, from that conversation I had with Nancy the next day.

Craig showed up EXACTLY as I requested. He was married and was very committed to his family so there was no chance of my creating a romantic relationship where he would rescue me and keep me from working through my own wealth mindset issues. He was irresistibly magnetic to money and was the perfect person to show me how to energetically address my financial dilemma. We had a really strong connection and became great friends really quickly. I could help him in a way that came naturally to me and he has told me numerous times that I am a tremendous gift to him, in ways he could never repay. On top of it all, we share a birthday and I did the process on my birthday so, in a way, we were birthday gifts to each other.

The Transformation

You might remember that in the beginning of this chapter, I told you that I had been emotionally and financially devastated from the ongoing court and custody battles with my ex-husband. That was what made me realize that I had to address my wealth mindset and reclaim my power. It is funny how facing our personal inner "demons" in our life can help us find our "angels."

Without the experiences with my ex-husband, I never would have realized that I needed to transform my wealth mindset; I never would have summoned Craig into my life and I never would have claimed my power in the ways I am about to reveal to you.

Right now, as I write this, I am in the midst of a third custody battle where, for the third time in four years, my ex has petitioned the court for full custody. The first two times, I settled out of court and each time, I lost a little bit more time with my kids.

This time, however, I have spent 2½ years diligently working on reclaiming my power and transforming my mindset as a result of meeting Craig. Had it not been for my experiences with my ex-husband, I never would have known the amount of work I had to do at reclaiming my power. I would have lived out a dull, wanting existence, not realizing how much power I had given away to the idea that I was lacking anything. In that way, my ex-husband is my angel because my greatest challenge has produced my greatest growth.

As we moved into this court battle, I knew that I wanted psychological evaluations for myself, my two daughters, my ex-husband and his new wife. This is not yet settled. However, I feel far more confident and self-assured than I have the previous two times we went to court over custody. I have been working on transforming my mindset for two years and along with that has come the money I needed to completely pay for these court-ordered psychological evaluations.

Had I still been living in victim mode and not been reclaiming my financial power, I never would have been able to pay for that. I feel more self-assured and confident that the outcome will be different this time, simply as a result of my transforming my mindset around money and reclaiming the power that I had given away.

I have discovered that my ex-husband is the real angel in this scenario. On some level, he loved me enough to force me to claim my power in ways I never imagined I would have to. That is the true gift in all of this and for that I am eternally grateful.

KERRI KANNAN (United States) is the author of *Uncovering the Divine Within* and the Founder of the *World Awakened Project*. With a focus on expanding consciousness through collaboration, cooperation and connection, the World Awakened Project offers a portal where leading-edge thinkers and leaders in the human potential movement offer guidance and support along your path of self-realization. Access tons of free gifts, coaching sessions, interviews and personal empowerment tools at HTTP://WORLDAWAKENEDPROJECT.COM.

KERRI'S FREE GIFT: 5 Keys to Conscious Creation Video Series PLUS Amazing Bonus Content at HTTP://EMBRACEDBYTHEDIVINE.COM/GET-YOUR-BONUS-GIFTS/

About Michelle Mayur,
Compiling Author

MICHELLE MAYUR, in partnership with the Divine, co-creates transfor-mational energetic shifts in women who are ready to make a bigger difference in the world. Through both her writing and her healing work, she assists women to dissolve limiting beliefs and energetic blockages so they can step fully into their Power, Passion and Purpose. Michelle assists women to anchor in the energy of the Divine Feminine in their life and work, embracing Compassion, Collaboration and Love, so that these heart-centered wayshowers can collectively birth the global vibrational shift towards more Peace, Harmony and Happiness.

She is a visionary leader, international speaker and the conscious en-trepreneur creator of the Heal the Healer community, WWW.HEAL-THE-HEALER.COM.

In 2012 she received the extremely powerful Goddess Isis Healing of Love™ energy healing system for personal and planetary healing as a powerful energetic download from the higher realms and now teaches this system widely.

After a transformational near-death experience in 1994 on the tiny equatorial island of Nauru, Michelle made a commitment to devote her life to helping others through her healing work.

Some of her professional highlights to date have included designing and facilitating several Spiritual Egypt Tours, which included group planetary healing work in such sacred locations as the Kings Chamber of the Great Pyramid, between the Paws of the Sphinx and in the Goddess Isis Sanctuary at Philae Temple. She has also run healing retreats in Bali.

Since 1995, Michelle has been running her successful healing practice, Angel Wings Healing, WWW.ANGELWINGS-HEALING.COM, seeing clients around the world, using her unique Goddess Isis Healing of Love™ energy healing system, angel-guided spiritual healing, mentoring and clinical

232 Embraced by the Divine

hypnotherapy. Her private global clientele includes company CEOs, Buddhist priests and Catholic nuns, to name a few.

A life-long learner, Michelle has a Science degree, as well as holding diplomas in clinical hypnotherapy, holistic healing, psychotherapy and qualifications in counseling, flower essences, disability, Sekhem and Seichim, as well as being a Reiki master.

Based in Melbourne, Australia, Michelle's loves – apart from her writing and healing work – are her two children, animal activism, spending time in nature, travel anywhere and everywhere, gardening and her pets. Every day she makes her meditation, spiritual practice and connection to nature a priority.

Connect with Michelle

MICHELLE@EMBRACEDBYTHEDIVINE.COM OR
HTTP://EMBRACEDBYTHEDIVINE.COM/CONTACT/

FACEBOOK: WWW.FACEBOOK.COM/MICHELLE.MAYUR

TWITTER: WWW.TWITTER.COM/EMBRACEBYDIVINE

LINKEDIN: WWW.LINKEDIN.COM/IN/MICHELLEMAYUR

Meet the Collaborators

*Michelle and all the Collaborators would love to have you
become part of the Embraced by the Divine Community at
www.facebook.com/EmbracedByTheDivineBook
You are invited to "Like" that Facebook Page too!*

JULIE ANN (Singapore – *The Gift of Feeling Intensely*) is an Intuitive Healer, Spiritual Coach, Workshop Facilitator, Creator of the "Seeing 11:11 – A Global Vision" daily intention project, and Author of the forthcoming book, *If You Are Looking for a Sign, This Is It!* Julie has facilitated workshops in Malaysia, Philippines, China and Australia as well as her home base of Singapore. She has created several online global intention projects and hosted events during various worldwide meditation gatherings. WWW.JULIEANN.CO

ANDREA BEADLE (United Kingdom – *Listening to the Voice Within*) helps heart-centered entrepreneurs find their purpose and create the business that is the expression of their soul. She believes that your business will only grow as far as you grow as an individual and, using Higher Guidance Coaching, helps you to break through the beliefs that are holding you back so that you can have a healthy life and a healthy business. She is creating the Heart Business Academy for heart-centered entrepreneurs at WWW.ANDREABEADLE.COM

RAELINE BRADY (Australia – *A Life in Metamorphosis*), is a dedicated Earth Worker and Gaian Midwife. She travels the world lecturing, teaching consciousness tools and facilitating retreat workshops to sacred power sites and with dolphins and whales. She is a vibrational essence developer and writer. Raeline is a Master Teacher of Usui, Tibetan and Karuna Reiki, Seichim / Sekhem and her own healing system, Radiance Force. WWW.SOUL-QUINTESSENCE.COM. Receive complimentary light language activations, empowering star elder wisdom and guided visualizations by following the Soul Quintessence Page on Facebook.

REV. LORRAINE COHEN (United States – **Getting Raw – Bungee Jumping into the Abyss**), is internationally recognized for one heart coaching, inner grace healing and higher light channeling. A fierce advocate for her clients' transformation, she uses her spiritual, intuitive, and healing gifts to support women to dive deeply into self–love, transmute emotional wounds and strengthen their personal connection to God to create a bold, abundant, and meaningful life. She is an international best-selling co-author, Unwavering Strength, Vol. 2 and writes for BellaMia Magazine. WWW.LORRAINECOHEN.COM

HELAINE Z. HARRIS, LMFT, (United States – **Survive to Soar – Becoming a Financial Phoenix**) empowers heart-centered clients to transform their lives and businesses to reflect their authentic selves, helping people to magnetize love, power, abundance and the right clients. An intuitive business coach, shamanic healer and psychotherapist, she is founder of An Awakening Center www.ANAWAKENINGCENTER.COM. With 35 years of experience and mastery of energy, she has helped thousands of clients. Author of the award-winning book, *Are You in Love with a Vampire? Healing the Relationship Drain Game.* WWW.HZHARRIS.COM

KERRI KANNAN (United States – **The Gift of Adversity**) is the author of *Uncovering the Divine Within* and the Founder of the *World Awakened Project*. With a focus on expanding consciousness through collaboration, cooperation and connection, the *World Awakened Project* offers a portal where leading-edge thinkers and leaders in the human potential movement offer guidance and support along your path of self-realization. WWW.WORLDAWAKENEDPROJECT.COM

REV. SAGE TAYLOR KINGSLEY-GODDARD, CHT, RM, (United States – **In the Hands of Angels**) known as The Prosperous Goddess™, is a 6-figure Intuitive Abundance Acceleration Coach, Archangel Michael channel, shamanic Intuitive Miracle (I AM) healer, Reiki Master and Teacher, and a dynamic catalyst for personal and planetary transformation. Acclaimed author of *The Radical Self-Love Guidebook* and the creator of "Angelic Abundance

Activator," voted #1 WORLD'S BEST LAW OF ATTRACTION PROGRAM, Sage passionately empowers heart-centered women to manifest more love & abundance! WWW.ANGELICABUNDANCEACTIVATOR.COM WWW.PROSPERITYPASSIONPURPOSE.COM

CHRISTINE KLOSER (United States – *The Best "Worst Time" of My Life*) is known as The Transformation Catalyst, is a spiritual guide, award-winning author, and transformational book coach whose spot-on guidance transforms the lives of visionary entrepreneurs and authors around the world. Her coaching and training programs have impacted more than 55,000 authors to help them unleash their authentic voice and share their message on the pages of a book. WWW.CHRISTINEKLOSER.COM

MICHELLE MAYUR (Australia – *Who Am I to Shine?*), in partnership with the Divine, co-creates transformational energetic shifts in women who are ready to make a bigger difference in the world. She assists women to dissolve limiting beliefs and energetic blockages so they can step fully into their Power, Passion and Purpose. She is the founder of the Heal the Healer community, WWW.HEAL-THE-HEALER.COM. Since 1995, Michelle has been running her successful healing practice, Angel Wings Healing, WWW.ANGELWINGS-HEALING.COM, seeing clients around the world, using her unique Goddess Isis Healing of Love™ energy healing system, angel-guided spiritual healing, mentoring and clinical hypnotherapy.

LINDA MURRAY (*Pee Wee, My Kelpie Mate*) lives in Australia after migrating from New Zealand. Whether city or country, nature is large in her life. Linda develops your understanding of nature messages given through weeds, bugs, disease, and animals. Choose earth-friendly ways and energies for step-by-step soil nutrition and health. Healthy soil is our legacy, our lifeblood and conduit to health. WWW.CARBICULTURE.COM is her knowledge hub and has lots of free advice. Linda shares how "dancing with nature" is a balancing act.

JOANNE NEWELL (Australia – ***Back to Health***) knows, to the depths of her soul, that enlightened, spirit-driven entrepreneurial women are here to change the world. They're here to live a full, rich life, and to help others and the planet. She also knows that money makes it possible for them to do all of this, so she helps women create an empowered money mindset. She reveals how to create a rich life, by design (in co-creation with Spirit). If you'd like to start creating a money mindset that works for you, then Joanne's here to help. WWW.RICHLIFEBYDESIGN.COM

JESSE ANN NICHOLS GEORGE (United States – ***If Only I Knew Then What I Know Now***), is a radio show host, the author of four books founded on the principles of compassion, and how to use it to bring joy to all areas of life, and to open to living your passion and manifesting a life of joy and fulfillment. She created The Genesis Clearing Statement and The Compassion Tour. Jesse is a Code Interpretor with over 33 years of experience working with clients and assisting others with their life processes. She is a 13th generation spiritual healer and Druidic practitioner WWW.JESSEANNNICHOLSGEORGE1.COM

JANET PARSONS (Australia – ***Open Your Mind and Say Ahhhhhhhh – Steps to Capsize a Crisis***) is an award-winning writer of stories and songs, with most ideas coming in at 3 a.m. when other people are sleeping soundly. The youngest of 13 children, she believes her imagination was fed by a healthy diet observing the antics of her siblings and being fuelled with great literature in a TV-free home. She lives in magnificent Melbourne, Australia, with her husband and children. Janet is currently working on her third children's book, a non-fiction novel and the first in a fiction series. Twitter: @potorooprose, blog: WWW.POTOROOPROSE.WORDPRESS.COM

BRENDA PEARCE (Canada – ***Lovingly Letting You Go***) is a Registered Nurse, author, artist, broadcaster, speaker, teacher, CEO E Factor Live Broadcasting and VP Customer Service at SR Broadcasting. Of all of these things, her greatest accomplishment is being mom to Kevin, James, Allison, and her beautiful angelic son Kenny, her four beautiful children. You can connect with her in many ways: E Factor Radio Network: WWW.EFACTORLIVE.COM. E Factor Live on Blog Talk Radio WWW.BLOGTALKRADIO.COM/EFACTORBRENDAPEARCE

DEB SCOTT, BA, CPC (United States – ***Grieving the Loss of the Illusion of Myself***) is a four-time award-winning author of, *The Sky is Green & the Grass is Blue* (**a Kindle Top 20 Best Seller!**), a top-rated best podcaster winner for, The Best People We Know Show, with over 1 million global listeners, and a Top 1% Kred Social Media Influencer. Deb battled dysfunctional relationships, depression, was the sole caregiver to both her parents who fought cancer to their death, and even experienced financial devastation. Deb helps people turn things around in their business and life. WWW.DEBSCOTT.COM

THERESE SKELLY (United States – ***How I Lost My Money and Found My Spirit***) is a money mindset mentor and business coach who works with heart-centered entrepreneurs who are ready to grow their business in a much easier and more authentic way. Blending her background as a psychotherapist, strategist, and business consultant, she masterfully works both the inner game challenges and the outer game tactics. From newer business owners to already successful entrepreneurs, Therese works with individuals who desire to make a big difference in the world. WWW.HAPPYINBUSINESS.COM

REV. EDIE WEINSTEIN, MSW, LSW (United States – ***Authenticity – Revealing the Real***) is a colorfully creative journalist, dynamic transformational speaker, licensed social worker, interfaith minister, radio host, bereavement specialist, addictions counselor, PR Goddess, Cosmic Concierge, BLISS (Brilliant Insightful Loving Safe Service) coach and the author of *The Bliss Mistress Guide to Transforming the Ordinary into the Extraordinary.* An *opti-mystic,* she views the world through the eyes of possibility. WWW.OPTI-MYSTICAL.COM & WWW.VIVIDLIFE.ME. It's All About Relationships radio show, Thurs. 8 pm EST.

FREE Gifts and Resources from the Author and Collaborators

Claim More than $2,100 Worth of FREE Gifts:

HTTP://EMBRACEDBYTHEDIVINE.COM/
GET-YOUR-BONUS-GIFTS/

JULIE ANN – Time for You – eBook and Meditation

ANDREA BEADLE – Audit Your Life eBook

RAELINE BRADY – 10% Discounts on Selected Soul Quintessence Products & Services

REV. LORRAINE COHEN – Creating a Magical Life Power Tools

HELAINE Z. HARRIS – Meet Your Prosperity Guide Package

KERRI KANNAN – 5 Keys to Conscious Creation Video Series PLUS Amazing Bonus Content

REV. SAGE TAYLOR KINGSLEY-GODDARD – Love Yourself Abundant Angelic Gift Set

CHRISTINE KLOSER – Free Audio Training for Budding Authors

MICHELLE MAYUR – How to Receive Angelic Guidance in Business and Life – 2 audio series

LINDA MURRAY – Sally My Teacher eBook

JOANNE NEWELL – The 3 Foundations of an Empowered Money Mindset – 3-part video series

JESSE ANN NICHOLS GEORGE – Genesis Clearing Statement – Have the Life You Truly Desire

JANET PARSONS – The Five Senses of Love Competition

BRENDA PEARCE – 5 Days of Distance Reiki Love & Support

DEB A. SCOTT – Mind Vitamin Minutes eBook

THERESE SKELLY – Mindset Mastery eBook

REV. EDIE WEINSTEIN – It's All About Relationships Radio Shows

If you have enjoyed and have been inspired by this book, you are warmly invited to LEAVE A REVIEW ON AMAZON to help spread the word.

BUSINESS 🎓 SCHOOL

Best Practice Business School is Australia's
own 'Harvard' for Small Business.

Our Mission
*Every day we help Business Owners to move from where they
are now to where they really want to be.*

**Come and learn how we are redefining entrepreneurship,
in a supportive community of business owners and
entrepreneurs just like you.**

www.bestpracticebusinesscoaching.com.au